T0167668

ENIGMAS & ....
An Anthology of Commonwealth Writing

Enigmas & Arrivals

An Anthology
of Commonwealth Writing

....

EDITED BY
ALASTAIR NIVEN AND MICHAEL SCHMIDT

CARCANET

First published in Great Britain in 1997 by
Carcanet Press Limited
4th Floor, Conavon Court
12–16 Blackfriars Street
Manchester
M3 5BQ

A CIP catalogue record for this book
is available from the British Library.
ISBN 1 85754 314 9

The publisher acknowledges financial
assistance from the Arts Council of England.
Publication of this anthology has
been sponsored by the Commonwealth Foundation.

Set in Sabon by Ensystems, Cambridge.
Printed and bound in England by SRP Ltd, Exeter.

CONTENTS

PREFACE

The term 'Commonwealth writing' has been under assault for at least a decade. 'Post-colonial literature', 'international writing in English', 'the new literatures', these and other sobriquets are endlessly proposed as alternatives to a term which for many carries a whiff of Queen-centred Anglophilia. It is sad that this should be so, because the word 'Commonwealth' has strongly radical origins, used in Shakespeare almost interchangeably with 'society', and adopted by the first constitutionalists of Massachusetts and Australia as a description of their new political status. As this anthology also demonstrates, there is a commonwealth of talent in the world of English-language books which makes the term 'Commonwealth literature' punningly appropriate.

This collection celebrates a major literary prize, now ten years old. The Commonwealth Foundation invented it and has commendably sustained it. The Commonwealth Writers Prize judges strive to find not only the best novel in English from Commonwealth writers in the previous year, but also the best first novel. Literary awards are often criticised for focusing only on the already discovered and sometimes already well-rewarded author. There is no danger of the Commonwealth Writers Prize doing this, since it is bound each year to confer recognition on four first-time novelists from different areas of the world. Some, like Louis de Bernières, may go on to win the Best Book category, but nothing will ever quite exceed the elation of that first moment when a writer knows that he or she has been read, admired and honoured across continents.

The Commonwealth Writers Prize must be one of the most complex awards to administer because it necessitates four juries convening in different quarters of the world to consider fiction entries from Africa, Australasia, the Caribbean and Canada, and from Europe and the Indian sub-continent. Distinguished judges from these vast chunks of the planet each select a winning novel as Best Book and as Best First Book, making a total of four winners in each of the two categories. To reach thus far is achievement enough and means that each of the selected books has won a regional prize, with money, honours and publicity. An international team of judges, drawn from all four sectors of the Commonwealth, next chooses overall winners in both categories. These winners receive another monetary award. Some of the writers who have won sections of the Commonwealth Writers Prize are represented in this book with four of those who have won what is informally known as the 'overall prize'. Collectively they provide us with a representative collage of the new fiction in English.

Where does this writing come from and where is it going? The flexibility of the English language is generic, for it is born out of the amalgamation of many different linguistic strains: Anglo-Saxon, Latin, Norse and Teutonic, among others. No other world language has been able to transplant itself so easily and then to absorb the characteristics of the area in which it is newly nurtured. Elements of non-European tongues readily instil themselves in the imported language, colouring it to such a degree that it may eventually be a virtually separate vernacular. We perceive hints of this in most of the writers in this book. In time the process leads to separately identifiable literatures, Australian, Canadian, Caribbean, Indian, as independent of metropolitan British writing as American literature is. Within each of these national identities lies further particularities: Olive Senior, for example, is not just West Indian but specifically part of Jamaican culture.

Parallel developments of language and cultural self-confidence are often expressed through parallel personal odysseys. Commonwealth writing is partly a story of migrancy and re-settlement. We see it in almost every writer in this collection: Lindsey Collen, South African long established in Mauritius; Adib Khan, Bangladeshi settled in Australia; Pauline Melville, Guyanese in London; Alex Miller, Londoner 'down under'; Rohinton Mistry, Indian in Canada. All the writers travel a great deal and some have made observation of other places a central feature of their major work.

This is a celebratory anthology, and we hope that it serves the practical purpose of introducing readers to some writers they may not yet know and to rich areas of world literature which for them may be unexplored. Every reading experience contains within it the enigma of discovery and a moment of arrival when the book falls into place within one's ever-interpreting mind. Ama Ata Aidoo, John Cranna, Githa Hariharan, Adib Khan are individual voices less heard in Britain than they deserve. Louis de Bernières, Rohinton Mistry, Mordecai Richler and Vikram Seth (author of perhaps the longest novel in English ever written), are best-selling authors. This anthology is not, however, built upon status or reputation but on the premise that good writing breeds its own equality. Anthologies are expressions of this. Each writer in *Enigmas and Arrivals* is outstanding. Together they are formidable.

The Commonwealth Writers Prize is ten years old but the phenomenon of Commonwealth literature has its roots in the last century. As we approach the year 2000, these writers help us to take stock of a migratory world without authoritative centres and where no one can be legitimately marginalised. Writers form their own centres and at the moment when we read them they are at the fulcrum of our personal experience. Reading is an enigmatic process, but through it we arrive at revelations of ourselves.

Alastair Niven
Michael Schmidt

Ama Ata Aidoo

ABOUT THE WEDDING FEAST

(*With a little warning for all those who may be allergic to the genre: that this is 'kitchen literature' with a vengeance – AAA*)

It had began with the announcement itself. That those two were going to get married. My granddaughter just came in from her workplace one early evening and told us. No asking. It was all telling. That was when something hit me. Yes, from that early. That there was something not right already. In the old days, when things were done properly, a girl did not just announce that sort of thing in that sort of way. But later, when I pointed out to the child's mother, my daughter Mary, she said that things have changed.

. . . Hei, and how they have changed! . . . And of course, being my daughter Mary, hard as a palm kernel outside and coconut-soft inside, she later came and without apologising for speaking like that to me, asked me how the young lady should have informed us about what she and her young man intended . . .

And then there was the matter of the time. How can a serious discussion like marriage intentions start at the end of the day? In the old days, if a young woman wanted to bring up such a matter, she would begin by just hinting one of her mothers on her mother's side, who would hint her mother, who would then have hinted me her grandmother, and then I and her mother would have discreetly mentioned it to any other mothers and grandmothers whom we considered close enough to be brought into the discussions and the negotiations that would follow. Then, very early the next morning – at dawn really – we would have had a meeting, in my room certainly, sitting down properly, of course ... But here I go again, forgetting that things have changed! In this case, the young lady came to just tell us. And that was how everything got handled. In the modern, educated way, and not at all properly.

Maybe, I should not have let myself grieve: since for a start, we were in a foreign land. The young man my granddaughter was going to marry is from one part of Africa that is quite far from our country. My daughter Mary had sent me a ticket to go and visit her and her husband and children. Indeed, let me tell the truth: when it comes to such gestures, Mary is good ... so I had gone. As everybody knows, this was the second or third time. In fact, I was preparing to return home here when the announcement came from my grandchild. That was a blessing. Because, the way things have changed, I could sense that they were going to go ahead and finalise everything, when no one at home had the slightest knowledge about the proposed marriage. And then, what was I going to tell everybody when I came back? You would all have laughed at me, no? That I too had gone and lost my head abroad: the way all these educated people seem to do when they travel overseas.

So I said to Mary my daughter: 'Mary, it is true that things have changed, but have they really changed that much?'

'Maybe not, Mother ... you only worry too much,' was what she said. Now tell me, what kind of a response was that?

Anyway, that was when I came back here and informed you all about it. I had been quite surprised and very relieved that you had all been so understanding. Was it you or Abanowa who had suggested that since the child was in a foreign land anyway, and the young man she was marrying does not come from anywhere around here, everybody should accept that there was no question of anybody getting the chance to go and check his background to make sure everything about him and his family was satisfactory, and so if I found him acceptable, that should be fine with you all? At the time, I had not commented on it, but oh, I was so grateful for that.

As I had informed you all at the family meeting, I knew Mary was going to be sending me a ticket to go back there for the wedding. But she had sent it much earlier ... Mary doesn't know how to do a lot of things. In that she is not alone. It's the education. It takes away some very important part of understanding from them ... But then, I must also say for Mary that those things she knows how to do, she does them very well.

So, that was how I came to be present at the big meeting between Mary and the boy's mother about what should be prepared for the wedding feast . . . To tell the truth, I had not really felt too happy at the idea of a joint discussion. It was not right. What self-respecting family in the old days would ask for help from their prospective in-laws? Whether it was in the way of just ideas or for something more substantial like the actual preparation of the food for the wedding feast? But when I so much as opened my mouth, Mary said that these days, that is not only all right, but even expected. She added that in fact, she might hurt feelings if she didn't ask for the help. Mmm, things have really changed, haven't they?

Since there was not going to be any grandmother from the boy's side at the meeting, Mary and I agreed that I would sit in on the discussions, but would keep a respectable silence. Which is what I did. However, every now and then, my daughter whispered questions to me to which I gave discreet answers.

It had not seemed as if there was much disagreement about anything. They had discussed everything in a friendly way: the wedding cake itself; other cakes; biscuits and buns; how to do the peanuts and the other things for the guests to munch and crunch . . .

Peanuts? O yes, they are everywhere! . . .

They had sat and talked for a long time, may be for as much as half the day, when they came to the foods that called for real cooking. That was when things began to take time to decide. I had been thinking, and even told them, that if they did not stop for a little rest and get something to eat, something nasty was going to happen. But Mary said, and it was plain the boy's mother agreed with her, that it was better to finish everything at a sitting. I was going to open my mouth and tell them that since the beginning of creation, no family had finished planning what should go into a wedding feast at one sitting. But then I remembered that things had changed, and warned my lips.

Then it happened and I was not at all surprised. I had heard Mary mention jolof and other dishes from our country. Then maybe, for just the shortest bit of time, I had got lost in my own thoughts and had not paid attention to the discussions. Because I had not noticed that something had come up which was really cutting their tempers short. All I saw was suddenly, Mary and the boy's mother standing up at the same time and each of them shouting:

'That's no food and you are not serving it at my daughter's wedding.'

'That's no food and you are not serving it at my son's wedding.'

'Spinach stewed with a mixture of meat and fish?' shouted one with a sneer that was big enough to wither a virgin forest.

'Spinach stewed with only onions and without meat or fish?' shouted the other, the contempt in her voice heavy enough to crush a giant.

'What do you mean?' shouted one.

'What do you mean?' countered the other.

'I said that's no food, and you are not going to serve it at my child's wedding!' they both screamed at the same time.

'You cannot tell me that,' one wailed.

'You cannot tell me that,' the other whined after her.

'Our guests will not eat that,' one spat out.

'Our guests will laugh at us if you serve that,' said the other.

'They will tell everyone in our community.'

'They will write home to everyone in our country about it.'

'It is awful, a mess.'

'Yours is unclean.'

'Yours is completely tasteless.'

'But you ate it when you came to our house!' said one, perplexed.

'But you ate it when you came to our house!' said the other, equally perplexed.

'No, I didn't. I didn't touch it,' they both confessed.

'Eh?!'

'I went and threw it into the rubbish bin in the kitchen.'

'W-h-a-t?'

They made as if they were going to clutch at each other's throats.

'Mother, Mother, what is this?'

None of us who were already in the room had seen or felt my granddaughter and the young man come in. But they had.

'What is this?' they repeated. The mothers stopped dead. Shame on their faces, each stared at the girl and the boy in the hallway. For what seemed to be a very long time, there was complete silence. Then the boy and the girl looked at one another, burst out laughing, didn't stay to say anything else to anybody and then went out of the room, still laughing.

What did the mothers do? What could they do? Each of them

just sat down and stayed sat. And quiet. After some time, I called my daughter Mary's name.

'What is it?' she asked, glaring at me.

'Listen,' I said, my voice low. 'I think you people had better stop now and continue with the planning of the feast tomorrow.'

'What is there to plan? . . . Anyway, I am finished with all that,' Mary said. And with that she went out of the room.

And that's how everything ended with the food affair. O yes, there was a wedding. And it was not only the ceremony itself that went well. Everything else was wonderful. We cooked our palaver sauce of spinach with egusi, meat and fish. The boy's people cooked their very plain spinach, without meat or fish . . . And did the guests eat? Don't even ask. They ate and ate and ate and ate. Since then, I have not heard that anyone from the boy's side complained about the food we cooked. And I am not hearing anyone from our side complain about the food our in-laws cooked . . .

You see o . . . what still puzzles me is how people can tell others how much things have changed, when they do not prepare their own minds to handle such changes, eh?! . . . And as my mother used to say: 'What is food anyway? Once it goes down the throat . . .'

Louis de Bernières

STUPID GRINGO

Jean-Louis Langevin strolled away from the Gold Museum, and reflected that Bogota was not quite as he had been led to expect. Someone in the office back home in Paris had said 'They call it the city of eternal spring,' and so Jean-Louis had arrived in the expectation that cherry trees would be in blossom, daffodils would be nodding in the parks, and beautiful tropical girls would be out and about in partial states of undress. He sniffed the moist air, with its bouquet of carbon monoxide and gasoline, and was reminded that much of any spring actually consists of gentle and persistent drizzle. At any rate, this was apparently the main ingredient of the allegedly eternal spring of Santa Fe de Bogota. It had been raining in a desultory fashion for three days, ever since he had arrived, and the beautiful tropical girls were effectively concealed beneath woolly sweaters, raincoats, and bright red umbrellas.

After three days he already felt like an old hand in South America, and laughed to recollect the wave of trepidation that had swept over him when his boss had come into the office one morning and announced that he was sending him to Bogota, with the idea that an office should be set up there, in order to market software packages all over the continent. Ideally, said the boss, such an office should be in a place like Rio de Janeiro, but the Brazilian currency had become exceptionally strong, making it too expensive to set up there, and Bogota was a fine cosmopolitan city with regular flights to every capital in Latin-America.

'But I don't speak Spanish,' said Jean-Louis, hoping to be excused from this particular mission, 'and I'm sure the Colombians don't speak French.'

'They all speak English,' said the boss, scrutinising him in an intimidatory manner, letting it be obvious that he had taken note of Jean-Louis' lack of enthusiasm. Jean-Louis began to blush. He certainly did not want to give the boss the impression that he was a laggard, or even a coward, but nonetheless some instinct of self-preservation made him say 'My English is very poor, as well, unfortunately. All I can say is "Where is the toilet?", "How do you do?", and "I love you".'

The boss laughed; 'The English only ever say "I love you" to their dogs. To each other they only say "Shall we have tea?"' The boss clasped an imaginary Englishwoman in his arms and gave her a cartoon kiss. 'O chérie,' he exclaimed, 'Let's go to bed and have tea.' The boss turned to Jean-Louis and said 'How the English have children, only the Good Lord knows.'

'It's virgin birth,' replied Jean-Louis. 'Perhaps it's more common as a miracle than one might suppose.'

'Anyway,' said the boss, 'they say that an Englishwoman can be tremendous as long as she's drunk. I was told this by a Greek. Englishmen are all homosexuals, of course.'

'Ah, Greeks,' repeated Jean-Louis, his mind drifting away to the terrible things he had heard about Colombia. What about that story that the police were exterminating the children who lived in the sewers? Jean-Louis seemed to remember that this had turned out to be a canard, a clever trick whereby an enterprising Colombian had screwed millions out of sentimental European charities. Well, what about all these political assassinations, and the kidnappings, and the violence of the cocaine mafia? He shuddered, and heard his boss saying 'When you get there, you are authorised to hire an interpreter.'

Jean-Louis suffered terribly in the three weeks before he went to Bogota. Everybody seemed to know a Colombian horror story. 'I hope you've made a will,' they would say, or 'I hope you're taking kungfu lessons,' or 'I think that you ought to confess and take the last rites before you go. Just in case.'

Everyone had some helpful advice, too; 'Don't walk in the backstreets even in daylight. If you hire a car, watch out for the people with guns who rob you whilst you're waiting at the traffic lights. If you travel out into the mountains, watch out for the bandits who hold you up at roadblocks. If someone approaches you in the street and talks to you, watch out for his accomplice who is behind you, picking your pockets. Don't go out wearing a watch, and don't take your wallet. Put your credit cards in your shirt pocket, and if you carry cash, roll it up and put it in your socks. Don't wear your wedding ring, but keep a couple of dollars on you so that muggers will be satisfied and leave you alone. If you don't give them anything, sometimes they stab you or shoot you out of pique, and they like dollars more than francs or pounds or pesos. And if you get stabbed or shot, you should refuse to have a blood transfusion because you might get Aids or hepatitis, so it's best to take a couple of litres of your own blood with you, and make sure that you also have your own hypodermic needles, because they tend to re-use old ones. And if you go to Barranquilla, watch out, because they've got the most virulent syphilis in the world. Oh, and another thing, "I love you" is "te quiero", and they don't lisp on the "c" sounds, as the Spanish do. So when you're in a bar you don't ask for a "thervetha" you ask for a "cerveza", O.K?'

Beneath this barrage of information, much of it delivered with overt smirks of schadenfreude, Jean-Louis began to feel like a condemned man, or like a workbench that has become dented from so many frequent blows of a hammer. He fell into a kind of agitated sadness, developed a valedictory attitude to the world, and allowed waves of nostalgia to wash over him. He remembered childhood holidays at the campsite at Luc-Sur-Mer. He remembered a Belgian girlfriend who had accompanied him on an expedition to Saumur, and an Englishman whose friendship he had lost, idiotically, after a quarrel about whether or not Bonaparte would have lost the Battle of Waterloo to the British, if the Prussians had not fortuitously turned up at a crucial moment.

Jean-Louis' wife noticed that he had become sad and wan, full of sighs and wistful glances, and so in the evenings she made him paupiettes de veau, and alouettes sans têtes, and pieds de mouton à la mode de Barcelonnette, in the knowledge that the blood draws up courage and optimism from the stomach.

Nothing could console him, however, on the evening of his last day in France. That afternoon he had heard scuffling and sniggering outside his office, and when he had gone out to investigate, he had found that his so-called friends and colleagues had taped a spoof obituary and a funeral wreath to his door. When he had returned to his computer terminal, and checked his E-mail for the last time, it had been full of mock tributes, such as one hears at a burial. That night Jean-Louis made love to his wife with tragical intensity, and lay afterwards with his head on her stomach, romantically listening to the gurgling of her insides, and feeling very much like a little boy in need of a mother's consolation.

But now, here in Bogota, he looked back at all that nonsense, and smiled. It was true that Bogota was actually somewhat cold and wet, and not in the least bit tropical, but every Colombian he had encountered had been charming, helpful, amiable, and rather shamingly cosmopolitan. Many of them spoke excellent French, in an accent that sounded strangely like Portuguese, and he had had several embarrassing conversations in which Bologna was compared to Seville, or in which Stockholm was compared to Venice. Jean-Louis had never been to most of the places in Europe about which Colombians seemed to be so enthusiastically knowledgeable, and on one occasion he had been forced to admit that he had not even seen the Pont Saint Pierre in Toulouse, or the monument to the Girondins in Bordeaux, and had never got round to seeing the version of the Mona Lisa that was hanging in the Louvre. Colombians seemed to be very fond of poetry, too, and he had had to bluff his way through discussions about Baudelaire and Prévert.

Yes, the Colombians were charming. He had not had to eat in his hotel even once, and had received more invitations to people's homes than he could possible honour. The cuisine had surprised him; he had been told that he would be eating llamas and guinea pigs marinaded in spices that burned holes in the oesophagous, but actually the cuisine was wholesome and even a bit bland. Chicken with rice seemed to be the ubiquitous favourite, and it did not even contain any garlic. Fried slices of banana were much better than one had any right to expect, and yucca had turned out to be delicious.

Jean-Louis felt relaxed in Bogota. His stomach was contented, the weather was like Paris at the beginning of April, and the bandits at the traffic lights were either cleaning car-windows, just as at home, or selling copies of *La Prensa*. Some of them appeared to be earning a living by selling the novels of Gabriel García Márquez, referred to familiarly as 'Gabo', so that at first Jean-Louis had thought that people must be unaccountably preoccupied with the actress who had just wanted to be alone.

It was true that his new Colombian friends kept warning him about the muggers – they had this strange gesture that meant 'Watch out for thieves', which consisted of pulling down one corner of the right eye with the forefinger – but it seemed to him that there was no sign of danger from anyone anywhere. The centre of the city was small enough to explore with the aid of a tourist map, and he had devoted happy hours to tourism that should have been spent exploring the possibilities for opening up an office for the marketing of software in Latin America.

Jean-Louis Langevin had been sensible, of course. He had put his credit cards in his shirt pocket, he had rolled up his cash and put it into his sock, where the notes chaffed him somewhat as he walked, he had left his watch and wedding ring in the hotel safe, and he had put a couple of US dollars in his trouser pocket so that any mugger could be sent away moderately gratified. Nonetheless, he was beginning to think that all these precautions were somewhat otiose, and that all the warnings and horror stories were simply the exaggerations of the inexperienced. He strolled away from the Gold Museum and back towards his hotel, admiring the sharp peaks of the mountains, and savouring the shafts of golden sunlight that were beginning to slice their way through the dirty grey clouds. 'Ah, at last, eternal spring,' thought Jean-Louis.

When he heard the footsteps behind him, though, approaching at a rate that was faster than a normal everyday walking pace, it was as if somebody had pressed a little button inside him. It was a button that switched off the sunlight, the mountains, the rainbow above the cathedral, the happiness of a casual tourist with time to waste. It was a button labelled 'fear', and suddenly all of Jean-Louis' senses went on the alert. Intently he heard the virile tapping of metal-tipped leather soles on the paving slabs. He smelled the scent of arepas frying in corn oil on the corner of the street. He tasted wet air in his mouth. His eyes rolled in an attempt to see behind himself without turning his head, and he felt a trickle of sweat abruptly course down the centre of his back and disappear into the waistband of his trousers.

'Hey, gringo,' called a voice behind him, and he flinched. 'Walk fast and don't turn round,' he told himself, 'act confidently and as if you know where you're going.'

'Hey hey, gringo,' came the voice again, and he increased his pace. It might just be one of those importunate hopefuls who wants you to help him find a job in Europe. He had had to cope with one or two of them already.

'Gringo,' called the voice again, this time with a clearly discernible note of irritation, 'gringo gringo gringo.'

Wasn't 'gringo' an insulting sobriquet for a yank? 'If he just wants to insult me, then I won't stop,' thought Jean-Louis, who certainly bridled at the thought of being mistaken for an American. The man was not saying it in an insulting fashion, however. It sounded vaguely friendly, perhaps even ironic.

Jean-Louis finally could not prevent himself from glancing behind, and he caught the eye of a large man in his early thirties. He glimpsed a yellow shirt with thin red pinstripes, grey trousers which were a little too tight about the thighs, and brightly polished leather shoes with ornamental buckles. 'Colombians,' he thought, his anxiety causing his mind to operate at hazard, 'always have nicely polished shoes.' The man was dark, like a Corsican, and seemed to be well-muscled and fit. 'Merde merde merde,' thought Jean-Louis, and he redoubled his pace.

'Momentico, momentico,' exclaimed his pursuer, 'espera. Mierda. Ay hombre, espera.'

Jean-Louis's mind went blank, and he made no sense at all of these Castilian exclamations.

There are only two types of person in such an emergency, the fleers and the fighters. Jean-Louis spontaneously discovered that in his case the response was definitely flight. Reason skidded away like a car on ice, and he broke into a run. Some extraordinary inhibition prevented him from calling for help; he was actually embarrassed to yell 'Au secours' in a Spanish-speaking country, and how can you yell 'help' in English, when you are French, and French people naturally cannot pronounce an 'H' even when there is no crisis?

'Hijo de puta loca,' he heard behind him as the man also broke into a run, 'Cabrón. Gringóncho. Espera.'

Jean-Louis ran, his feet blurring beneath him, and a copious cold sweat breaking out all over his head. He smelled his own rancid panic, and felt his eyes bulging painfully. Behind him he heard the steady and inexorable tapping of metal toecaps on stone, and the perspiration ran down into his eyes, blinding him. He wasn't sure, but it seemed to him that tears were coming from his eyes and mingling with the sweat. He wanted to pray, to call upon God or the Virgin, but all he could come up with, like a blasphemous litany, was 'salaud salaud salaud salaud'.

Jean-Louis blundered on, cannoning off lamp-posts and astonished pedestrians, fending off stacks of cardboard boxes, overturning dustbins, whilst behind him the terrifying and implacable steel toecaps drew ever closer.

Jean-Louis felt a squeal emerging from his throat, like the sound of an injured pig, or a woman keening over a death, and realised quite suddenly that all his strength had gone. It was the altitude; no stranger can run for very long at three thousand metres, even when that stranger regularly plays tennis at home in Paris. He felt his legs turning to rubber, and his feet increase in weight until they seemed to be pulling his knees to the ground. Nausea overwhelmed him, and his heart leaped and thumped in his chest like a beast that has been confined and is bound on breaking the bars. 'I'm going to die,' thought Jean-Louis, 'O God, I don't want to die.'

Expending a last desperate overdraft of strength, he turned right up a side-street, and ran straight into a dead end.

His hands spread out against the brick wall, Jean-Louis, blinded by tears and sweat, his lungs cramped and shredded, his legs shaking, decided officially that he was going to give up. He was not going to turn and run, and he was not going to turn and fight. He was going to turn around and allow himself to slide down the wall amongst the overflowing dustbins that suddenly seemed so inviting and enticing. To die and to sleep seemed to be much the same thing, and both seemed equally attractive. He was already sprawled amid the rubbish, weakly struggling to loosen his tie, when the man with the steel toecaps rounded the corner and stopped before him, panting a little, but not enough to prevent a radiant smile from creasing his face.

Jean-Louis looked up and saw an impressive row of white teeth, amid which there sparkled one that was made of gold. He saw sensual lips, dark brown eyes, an impressive and glossy black moustache, and a tawny skin that sprouted with thick and exuberant stubble. More thick hair sprouted from his chest where the top button of his yellow shirt was unfastened. He was not as big as Jean-Louis had first thought, but he had the stout and finely muscled forearms of a physically active man. Jean-Louis caught a fleeting impression of a chunky gold watch and several substantial gold rings.

The man reached down, and Jean-Louis whimpered and cowered, shielding his face with his arms. Mumbling in placatory desperation, he started to fumble hopelessly for the dollar bills in his trouser pocket, and thrust them towards the man with little nervous flicks of the wrist. 'Voilà, voilà,' he gasped, and the man took them from him. He looked them over with mystified attention, shrugged, shook his head, and then leaned down and stuffed them perfunctorily into Jean-Louis' shirt pocket, where they joined his credit cards.

The man reached into his own trouser pocket, pulled something out, and waved it in front of Jean-Louis' face. The latter cringed, fearing that it must be a weapon, perhaps a knife or a derringer. Again he crossed his arms in front of his face to protect it, still blinded by sweat and terror, and heard the man sigh with exasperation; 'Hijo 'e puta. Su dinero. Eh, gringo.'

In the midst of his fright, Jean-Louis became aware that the man was actually tickling him. He was brushing something lightly across the backs of his hands, and on the top of his head, mussing his hair. Whatever it was that he was being tickled with, it felt like crisp paper, and made a clean rustling noise like sycamore leaves on a dry autumn day. As his wits reassembled themselves, Jean-Louis began to realise that what the man was tickling him with, was a roll of banknotes.

He looked up incomprehendingly, and then, astonishingly, the man began to mime. He pointed down to his left foot, he raised it, he flexed the elastic around the top of his sock, he put the roll of banknotes into his sock, and then withdrew it again and dropped it on the ground. He mimed spotting it and picking it up, and then he mimed running, waving the roll in front of him.

All at once, understanding dawned upon Jean-Louis. His hand went down to his sock, and he felt the now empty place where his money had been concealed for safety. 'Mon argent?' he asked the man, and the man stuffed the money into his shirt pocket, along with the dollar bills and the credit cards. 'Su dinero,' explained the man again, gesturing towards the wad where it lay in its new place of concealment.

New tears began to follow each other down Jean-Louis' face. He would never know whether this was from relief, or gratitude, or from bitter shame. The man reached into his own pocket and produced a tooled leather wallet. Out of it he pulled all his money, the scribbled reminder notes, business cards, and credit cards. These he returned to his own trouser pocket, and then he reached into Jean-Louis' shirt and removed the latter's cards, cash, and token dollars. He tucked them into the empty wallet, and presented the wallet to Jean-Louis. 'Un regalito,' he said, his eyes twinkling, 'un recuerdo de Colombia. Con mis mejores deseos.'

Jean-Louis' confusion and horror were slowly beginning to

subside, along with the insupportable thumping of blood behind his eyes and in his temples, and he took the wallet in his hands and gazed at it with childish wonder. He looked up at the man who had decided to give it to him so that he would not have to carry his cash insecurely in his socks, and he began to laugh, his shoulders heaving, and his breath coming in painful sobs. The Colombian was momentarily nonplussed, but then he smiled, leaned forward, and patted Jean-Louis on the cheek. It was a gesture both paternal and patronising, a gesture full of humour and sympathy and affection. He patted Jean-Louis' face again, and came up with the only appropriate English words he knew; 'Estupid gringo,' he said.

Lindsey Collen

THE COMPANY I KEEP

'I must go see mom,' I think. 'Don't want them boarding her up.'

As I get into my bub-car, and press start, I have this premonition that I'm going to see something. That I'm maybe going to *come across* something.

Not a very nice thing either.

But *seeing* it is going to be inevitable.

I'm going to see this something, a something that I've caught sight of before. Three times before, to be precise. All in the last three weeks. This time will be the fourth time.

A fourth time.

And there will be no avoiding it.

I shiver.

'Nonsense!' I think.

Quite suddenly, I get a strange yearning for closeness. Just to be close to something living. Something warm. Perhaps the feeling of a heartbeat. *Lub-dub. Lub-dub.* The lull of someone's breathing near me. Now in, now out. Now in, now out. Or a gentle snoring. Maybe just a tender hand on my knee.

It passes.

The damned bub-car isn't starting.

So I sit and wonder. Mistake, this wondering. I end up wondering about the sight, a sight threatening to come back again today. To come screaming towards my bub-car at 220 kilometres an hour. Like everything else does.

At first, the first time I saw it, I thought it was a bunch of old sticks. A one-off thing. I don't even know how it caught my attention.

It was only three weeks ago. I was just going past in my bub-car. I had the compu-study-disk on as well, which usually excludes extraneous vision. But, it happened: I saw it: I caught sight of it out the corner of my eye. *A bunch of old sticks.*

It was just lying there, just outside someone's gate, by their air-meter.

Something sinister about it. 'Spooky,' I whispered to myself.

Didn't know what.

Of course, rubbish wasn't allowed to be visible. Maybe that was what was sinister about it.

I should have mentioned it to someone. But who? And what exactly would I have said anyway?

I'll have to press start again, because the bub-car isn't taking. Bad news. With this delay in starting, I find myself checking the internal air supply. That outdoor air hurts my nose and throat. I've got enough air to get me to mom's place and back again. Just. I've got a small air cylinder with me to give her as a present, as well. 'She'll love that. Always so worried about being in arrears.'

Here it comes again. This feeling of being in need. In need of warmth. A deep longing drags at my stomach, like periods. Somewhere between pleasure and pain. Probably because I was womb-born. One of the last, I was. That's probably how I'm left with this yearning.

'Thank goodness,' I exclaim, as the bub-car takes, and lurches forward. The acceleration, which is usually exciting, leaves me stone cold. I'm even a bit offended at its domination of my body, it, an object.

As I set off in my bub-car to see mom, I remember why it's today I'm going to see her.

It's her birthday. Lucky I'm bringing the air cylinder, it'll double as a birthday present. I'll buy a little something on the way, I think, to go with it. I think this while checking my credit card under the skin of my wrist. *Something old, something new, something borrowed, something blue.* What a silly rhyme to come into my head. Birth, marriage, death, I muse on mindlessly.

My credit card somehow sets me thinking about the next time I saw the bunch of old sticks, because I had seen it again. I had naturally got this feeling of *déjà vu*.

Déjà vu. And the sinister feeling of *déjà senti*.

You can't see the same formation of a bunch of old sticks twice.

You can't get the same feeling twice either.

And in different places.

The first one was very near where mom lives, in Labit, you know as you go along Desart Street. My mom once told me that there used to be a huge mango-tree there and a thing called a public fountain. Free water flowing, she claimed. Children drinking water, just like that. You just press on the top of the thing and water spurts out. The sound like a water-fall. Gushing. A spring. On the edge of the street. Laughing, she said, and touching one another's shoulders and holding hands, they were, the children. That was where it was, the old bunch of sticks. Just where the big mano-tree had stood. By where the public fountain had been.

The second one was near where I live in Nuvelvil. It was near to one of those VAT depots for people who owe money to all and sundry. Mainly for medical bills and insurance. Also for things like water, light and air. Nuvelvil, where I live, was built on the rocky soil of the northern plains, after the bankrupting of all the northern sugar-planters. I don't like living there. It's funny, but I don't like it. Where did the planters all go?

First, there was this campaign, mom said, to close down the Agro-Insurance Fund. Fraud, they said in Parliament, and corruption, they said in the press. True. So they closed it down. Then they set up this privatised planters' insurance. Which naturally went bankrupt after the next drought in the north. The planters took loans from the privatised banks. Which naturally fore-closed on them after the next drought and confiscated their land. Then Build-Operate-Transfer investors bought the land up, because they knew about the new airgar they would build there, and the new mass transit metro. So they built Nuvelvil. We are all still paying them. Me too. Every month. The rent rises relentlessly because it's attached to god knows what currency.

And it was quite near the local VAT depot, near here, that I saw the second one.

It was also just lying there. Like a bunch of old sticks. Like *the* bunch of old sticks. Just outside the gate. Of the local VAT depot, by its air-meter.

But I had already gone past in my bub-car before I realised that it couldn't be a bunch of old sticks, or even *the* bunch of old sticks.

One thing I don't like about bub-cars is the speed they go at.

I know it's unfashionable to say so, but I still agree with the

200-kilometre-an-hour speed limit in built-up areas for iron-steel-and-plastic vehicles. Who am I to mention how full the clinics are? How much money is made from maiming and killing? Who am I to mention all those expelled for not paying bills at the clinics? Who am I to tell of the money made by prostheses sales? From advertising campaigns for insurance and clinics and what not?

As I hurtle along, I don't put on anything to listen to or to study or anything.

I just hurtle.

Instead of feeling the same feeling of needing warmth, I now feel the rise of panic. Flight, or is it fight?

Emptiness.

Falling into it.

The others don't anymore. Don't feel anything, that is. Anything at all. They say feelings are on the wane. 'Old-fashioned,' they say. Expect them to be gone altogether, by the next generation. 'Left-overs of the womb,' they say. 'Cause sexual desires,' they say. 'Don't be hysterical!' the authorities say, referring to feelings. Any feelings are hysteria, they say.

And the strange thing is that there are these frequent outbursts of real hysteria. Mass hysteria. In lieu of feelings?

Who knows?

Again I go back to the premonition. I'm going to see another one today.

The next time I had seen one looming up, once again I was in my bub-car, again it was on the edge of the road. It was in Bo-Basin this time, by the Brown Sequard Rehabilitation of Debtors Centre, right by the air-meter again. I work there. At the Centre. I am one of the few remaining servants of the authorities. There's the police lifers, there's the VAT lifers, there's the magistrates and there's the debt-rehabilitators like me. Everyone else is stand-by. Wake up in the morning, put on the telecomputer, and see if your number comes up. If it does, you turn up. The work you get keeps you credit-worthy.

This time I just had enough time to see that it wasn't a bunch of old sticks at all. It was a totally different texture from a bunch of old sticks.

Not that I could see what it actually was, that is. I had already turned into the drive. You can't reverse there. So I made a mental note of it. But when I came out again after work, it was gone.

It had looked more like a twisted set of about three or four inter-linked cardboard boxes. Three or four cubes, touching one another at the pointed end of each cube. Corrugated cardboard boxes.

Again it had the air of something thrown away.

Discarded.

Rubbish.

Garbage.

Junk.

What made me put two and two together was that all three times, the air-meter people had boarded up a room.

In the same glance, I had seen, behind each of the bunches of old sticks or twisted cardboard boxes, that there was at least one boarded-up room.

The memory comes back right now as I'm on my way to mom's in Labit.

That is howcome there's this sinister feeling, I realise.

At the house in Labit, at the VAT depot, and at the Rehabilitation Centre, the sight represented an ending.

They boarded up your room when you didn't pay the Company your air bill. It was called Compagnie Générale de l'Air.

Two months and that was it. Boarded up you were. They were very strict. They put this kind of seal over your port-hole. And then, of course, you were a goner. And it was your own fault.

Air got privatised some ten years ago.

First just the Port Louis supply.

Then everywhere.

At first it was on condition that they wouldn't board you up if you didn't pay. Otherwise there would have been an outcry. Some people said this was the last straw. Others said it was inevitable. Ineluctable. Unavoidable. It had, they said, after all, happened over generations. The land had been privatised. Then the rivers. Then the water. Then the health. Then the sea.

The light supply had been a turning point. After oil, coal and gas had run out, they put up this satellite with a mirror on it. It orbited at a constant position relative to the land mass concerned, and produced constant light, and electricity, to all businesses and houses on a 24-hour-a-day basis. It was the only source of electricity. And the only source of light after dark. To get access to it, you had to put up port-holes, so that if you didn't pay your bills to the Company, they could board you up. So the boarding-up principle started long ago. With the privatisation of light. But of course, you could live, only just, without light. Specially in warm countries. There wasn't the problem of heating.

So when time came to privatise the air, there weren't too many arguments left. So, privatised air it is, they said. The only profitable way, most said. The only genuinely efficient way. The only way to prevent wastage. And maladministration. The only good investment, they said. Creates more number-calling. Good for the economy, they added.

Of course, I don't follow economic debates, you know. Nor politics really. I just get on with my job at the Debtors Rehabilitation Centre and go to see mom from time to time.

By then, by the time the air privatisation debate came up, the government was bankrupt in any case. What government wasn't? So if you want air, you have to buy it. Naturally. The outside air is so polluted, you get respiratory problems from the least exposure. So you have to buy good air. It only stands to reason.

All this is quite recent. As regards the air bills, the boarding-up itself must have started only about six months ago.

Time flies.

They just cancel you.

If you aren't creditworthy anymore, they tag you on the Identity Cards, and then in no time, you end up being a debtor. If you owe for two months, they just come and board you up. A total seal. I've got this friend who gets casual work at the seal factory, when her number comes up. They are air-tight, all right, those seals.

So they just board you up.

Then it's only a matter of time.

But then, at that time, six months ago, every person had his or her individuated Private Insurance money for their own cremation. Well they didn't have it really, being dead as doornails. They were grey, by the way, the colour of doornails, actually, having died after being boarded up. By suffocation, they wrote on the death certificates. They had it, the Individuated Private Insurance, when they were alive.

Death still left me with feelings, Feelings of intense sadness. A hollow grief. Loss. Encroaching loneliness. A giddiness into the back of time and into the abysm of space. A desire again to be near someone, some creature, perhaps fluffy and warm, maybe even with a nice cold nose like a puppy, maybe snorting gently like a pigling, maybe shivering like an albino rabbit in a cardboard box with its lettuce leaves. Maybe a horse, neighing in my arms.

I pop in at the delicatessen to get mom a little something to go with the air cylinder. I don't bother to use the cylinder myself, just rush in to the delicatessen.

I am rash. I buy her a rose. The man in the shop checks my wrist carefully on his meter.

'Creditworthy,' it pipes out in those awful monotones on these machines.

A strange feeling of rage rises up inside me. The only thing that came close to me had been the creditworthy machine, and this made me cross.

Mom once fell foul of the authorities, you know. Long long ago. She was very young. And apparently high-spirited. She was in some far-fetched movement against the privatisation of the sea. Yes, they all, everyone, creditworthy or not, used to get access to the beaches, she tells me. That was before the barbed wire and the hire-purchase-cubicles for non-tourists.

'You wouldn't believe the beauty,' she once told me, 'of the sun setting against the I'wento Ros rocks, how fast it fell into the sea. The spray,' she said, 'would rise up real slow and cause young people to want to kiss one another.'

Sounded very old-fashioned to me.

'I'll ask her for her recipe books,' I think aloud. 'Not that anyone cooks anymore.' She knew so much, or I think she did. I suppose she did. I feel I want to know. To understand. I am trying to control the rage that I have just quelled.

As I draw up in my bub-car, I am overwhelmed. All at the same time, there is the feeling of wanting to be close, the panic, the rage, they all join up in me.

And regret.

The regret gets mixed up with her recipe books.

Then I see it.

'No!' I cry.

There's a seal on her port-hole.

'No,' I cry again.

They've gone and done it, I think. They've boarded her up.

'Mom!' I cry out.

On deaf ears.

There's a bunch of old sticks – no it's the twisted set of four cubes, like corrugated cardboard by her door.

I hold my breath and get out of the bub-car. I'm pretty well trained at avoiding breathing too much outdoor air. I leave my hat on the dashboard. Holes in the ozone be damned. I put my hand up to bar the sun. It eats into my hand cruelly.

I walk over.

I see a note.

I read.

Do not touch. Debtor dead. Cause: suffocation. To be removed by the Compagnie générale de l'air (CGdA) for free incineration. R.I.P.

I go back to the bub-car.

I pull out the air cylinder and fix the thing to my face. I've held my breath enough. My fingertips are darkening. My eyes are burning somewhat from the air.

I pick up the rose and walk over to her. I know it's her, of course.

It's all so clear now.

I put the rose on the twisted boxes, twisted so as not to look like a coffin. Might offend. Rather leave her looking like an old bunch of sticks. By the air-meter.

My head is clear.

My feelings suspended.

The rose looks too dead. This offends me. I pick it up and tear its petals and leaves off one from another and throw them into the air, leaf by leaf and petal by petal, and they float, waft, and then settle. 'More like life,' I say.

I manoeuvre the door. Its seal gives. I push it in.

It opens. I take the mask off for one breath. Carbon dioxide. Colourless. Odourless. Dead.

'Ah,' I think. 'Not yet re-sold by the Housing Company. And some security guard's forgotten to lock it.'

A private company, naturally.

Inside is nothing, really.

The Housing Company has taken everything that can be sold. In lieu of debts, I assume. I see just one old pair of sheets and a filthy pillow. I am legally the heir. But the private civil courts are so costly that no one like me is an heir anymore.

I go and lean over the sheets and the pillow.

I take the cylinder off my face again and I put my face to the pillow. I take a deep breath. Never mind the carbon dioxide.

I smell the pillow. I want to smell the pillow.

This long-gone sense, olfactory they used to call it, comes back and I feel the world of memories, of generations.

The pillow smells of old-age and illness and death. But that is just on the surface.

Underneath, on the inside, is the beautiful smell of mom, herself.

Gentle perspiration. Long gone periods. A geranium leaf. Biscuits cooking in the oven. Guavas boiling to become jam. Rain on freshly cut grass. Milk flowing from her breast. Dough rising under a wet cloth.

And on one corner of the pillow-case is the most exquisite hand-woven embroidery. One thread thick. Roses. A cutting of a rose bush. Ready to plant. And petals. Petals floating. And the roots spider-web-like seeking water. Work done so efficiently. So perfect. And done free. Not for sale. Not for trade. Not for profit.

As I take the pillow-case off – I'm going to hide it, and keep it – I feel something slightly stiff inside it.

A tiny bundle of old paper.

Ah, I know what it is. Instinctively I shove it into my bra. My heart rustles against the recipes as it beats. Paper made by men and women from trees, close to me, trees planted by men and women, close to me, ideas passed from time immemorial by word of mouth, ideas then coded in this writing on this paper. Nestling to my breast. The pillow-case with this embroidery from time immemorial, of this plant cutting-by-cutting through time, on the other side of my bra, moving with my breathing.

I put my air cylinder on again.

I stand there for a long while. Breathing in and out in that dark, cold, airless house.

I go out and stand next to the air meter.

I pay homage to the old bunch of sticks and rose petals and leaves which are now mom.

A silent thought is the only ceremony she gets.

And it is in this moment that something in me is re-born. Maybe it did come out of mom, into me. Who knows? 'I'll join the others,' I think, 'if they'll accept me.' I only know one person in the movement. I don't even know its name. Or hers. Some people call it the movement against private theft of collective things. I call her 'The one who still laughs'.

'I'll go see her now.'

A light wind comes and blows the petals into the air, like a sigh, they hover, and then they settle on mom, nestle closer to her.

John Cranna

VISITORS

My Grandfather was a large man with a strong laugh who grew pomegranates for pleasure, but for reasons that only gradually became clear to me, and certainly were not clear to him, it was felt necessary from time to time to strap him to a bed and apply electric shocks to his head.

When I saw him after his treatment he had difficulty in recognising me, so I stood at his side for a while, repeating my name until the dullness had gone from his china-blue eyes. Although I was only fifteen, I was careful to arrange my face into a mask of apologetic innocence, in fear that he would begin to link my appearance with the treatment he was receiving. When the Pale Suits had gone away he would get up slowly and go out into the garden, where he would walk for a time, occasionally stopping at one of his fruit trees to touch the skin of a pomegranate that had hung there all summer, as though extracting its smooth permanence from the wreckage that had been made of his immediate past.

My grandfather had travelled in the time when this was still possible, and had collected musical instruments from around the Pacific. They stood in the dim corners of the house, or hung on the walls, a great Javanese gamelan in the hallway, and a Chilean lute on a shelf above. In the long afternoons when our

Visitors was a coalescence of a number of concerns I had at the time. Small Pacific nations were struggling to establish their identities in the face of stronger cultural forces. The region had become an arena for this kind of conflict. I had just read Noam Chomsky's persuasive work The Washington Connection and Third World Fascism. Closer to home, my father was a musician, who saw his art as a spiritual amulet against corrupting modernity. These were the hidden co-ordinates of the story.

visitors worked on my grandfather in the front room, I could hear the instruments in their other lives singing to me. The gamelan I knew well; it sat on the edge of a clearing in the jungles of Java, played by smooth-faced boys, its heavy sound mingling with the trees and the soil. The sound was very clear to me; it lodged in my chest as a kind of ecstasy, and it would only fade when the surge of voices from the front of the house told me that the men had finished with my grandfather. They went then to the kitchen and spoke to my mother, although I could never hear what they said to her. I watched from a window as they walked down the drive, two men in pale suits, one of them carrying an aluminium case, which was laid carefully in the back of the waiting vehicle.

The house and the garden were too large for the three of us who lived there, we had unused rooms, some still locked and containing the possessions of members of the family whose whereabouts were no longer discussed. On one side of the long hall that ran through the house my grandfather and I had our rooms, and on the other, at the furthest end of the hall, was my mother's room, a sanctum that no one was allowed to enter. My mother was a graceful person who moved about the house without ever seeming to touch it, and who each afternoon following lunch would brush my cheek with the lightest of kisses, before retiring to her room for the remainder of the day. After she had gone the long hall held a trace of her perfume, lingering there amongst the instruments, as though the house was reluctant to concede her departure.

At the edge of the orchard my grandfather sat and watched his pomegranates ripen, indifferent to passing showers. In a murmur that carried across the lawn to the house, he spoke endlessly of his years travelling the Pacific in search of instruments for his collection, struggling to prevent the treatment he was receiving from unravelling the thread of his memory forever. I sat beside him on the grass and tried to follow the path of his reminiscences. From Java and the jungles of Indochina it would lead suddenly east to Mexico, then south to the deserts of Chile, before veering west again to the island chains of Micronesia. A story that began in Djakarta might end in Santiago without his being aware that the location had changed, and fragments and characters from one tale would find their way into others, so that his monologues were jigsaws of confusion that held me entranced for hours, but which I could never fully understand.

Some things, however, were clear to me. He had always stayed among the ordinary people, whether it was in the shanty towns of the great cities or in the small, poor towns of the interior. He was obviously welcome in these places, and because of his enthusiasm for the music of the people, instruments would be produced and impromptu concerts arranged. He was often invited to join in the music-making and in this way he became a competent performer on dozens of the instruments he had collected. I could only dimly recall the times from my childhood when he performed for the family in the front room, but I have a clear memory of his large figure stooped forward slightly, playing a lute made from the shell of an armadillo, and holding it so carefully in his arms that he might have been cradling the shell of a massive rare egg. The lute, which was from Chile, now rested in the hallway, where it had remained untouched for many years.

One of my grandfather's remaining clear memories was of his time in Chile and he told me of the year he had spent there in the northern deserts, studying the ancient music of the Atacameno Indians. The language of their songs, he said, was so old that the performers did not understand it themselves, and he described the strange sound of the great side-blown trumpets that accompanied the performance. He had lived in the home of one of these musicians and he spoke of the stark beauty of the deserts and of the resilience of the people who had lived there since the dawn of time. One day, as we sat in the orchard, he told me with surprise in his voice that he had never been happier than when he was with the Atacameno, but when I asked him why he had left, his eyes dulled and his story slid off once more into confusion.

The men in pale suits were visiting twice a week now, and as I sat there beneath the fruit trees, I heard the quiet sound of their vehicle pulling up at the bottom of the drive. My grandfather fell silent at their footsteps on the gravel, and was suddenly very still in his chair. We could hear the Pale Suits talking with my mother, and then her breathless voice calling to us across the lawn. My grandfather got up and walked slowly towards the house, where our visitors would now be waiting for him in the front room. I waited for a while, then went into the hall and sat there in the gloom amongst the dead instruments. I concentrated very hard, until the loudest sound I could hear was the steady beat of the blood in my ears, then softly, across a great distance, I heard the strains of the lute singing in an Atacameno village, and the music grew stronger and more clear, until I was there among the scatter of low huts, listening to the lute as it cut the thin air of the desert. I saw my grandfather, dressed in the clothes of the Indians, working with them in their carefully irrigated fields on the desert's edge, and returning each night to study their ancient music in the household of a master musician. I saw him crouched by an oil lamp, taking down the music of an evening performance in his notebook, and writing out the unknown language that was used in the ritual songs of fertility and death. And then the lute began to sing of strange Indian tribes my grandfather had never mentioned, the Aymara and the Pehuenche; it sang of their languages, of their music, of the rich collection of myth that held together their pasts, and it sang of their struggle against the lethal promises of a new order that had come recently to their land. I was so absorbed by the tales of the lute that I almost missed the babble of voices from the front of the house that signalled the end of my grandfather's session, but the moment the Pale Suits opened the door into the hall, the lute fell silent again.

When the men were in the kitchen, speaking in their sing-song voices with my mother, I went in to see my grandfather. He lay on the bed, the straps loosened at his sides, staring up at the ceiling with unblinking eyes. An acrid smell hung in the room, and a circular stain lay around him on the sheet. I stood there for a while, listening as the kitchen door closed and our visitors' footsteps receded on the drive. I watched the stain spread out across the bed, and thought, They've embalmed him and the fluid is already beginning to leak out. His body seemed a long way off, as though it was withdrawing into the angles of the room, and I felt a sensation of falling. I put a hand out to the wall, and as I did so my grandfather turned his head to look at me, his face blank and his eyes empty of all life. He made a weak gesture with one hand. 'They're very kind to take so much trouble with me. I feel I should be more grateful . . .' I had never spoken to him about his treatment before, and now, hesitantly, I asked what they had decided was wrong. He frowned, as though trying to remember a complicated diagnosis that had once been fully explained, but eventually he shook his head and lay back, his eyes fixed once more on the ceiling. Behind me the door opened and my mother came into the room in a cloud of perfume. She opened the curtains with one hand while holding a handkerchief against her face with the other. 'What have you done, Father?' she said. 'You know you really can't behave like this in front of our visitors.'

That evening, as though in protest at my grandfather's lack of discretion, she failed to appear for dinner, so the two of us ate alone. Although he had bathed and changed his clothes, a faint odour still hung about him, and when I sat down to eat I found my appetite had gone and I could not bring myself to finish my meal.

It had been six years since my sisters and my father had gone away to the mountains. I was too young to understand at the time, but soon after that the schools closed down and before long the Pale Suits called at our house for the first time. My mother would not allow me to go into the city, so the only Pale Suits I saw on foot were the pair who came to visit my grandfather. At other times I saw them passing the house in their long vehicles, and always they were on the wrong side of the road, driving very fast. When I asked my grandfather about the Pale Suits in their vehicles, he was unable to tell me anything. He was fully occupied, it seemed, with his dissolving past, and the only energy he had left for the present was expended on his orchard. There his pomegranates hung thickly on the trees, the best crop there had been in years, he told me, and the fruit were at the point of cracking from within with their own ripeness.

My grandfather spent many hours in the orchard, inspecting the bark of the trees for disease and the leaves for the first signs of summer blight. Often he would stop and stare at a ripening fruit for a time, touching it with his open palm, before moving on to the next laden tree. The longer his treatment continued the more important the orchard became to him and sometimes he would call me over to a tree and explain his methods of soil preparation and pruning. It was important, he said, that there was someone to take over the orchard when he could no longer manage it. From the bottom of the orchard I could see the outline of the distant mountains, and I began to watch them more closely, thinking of my sisters and my father, trying to imagine them eating and sleeping somewhere among that jumble of pale shadows.

On the next occasion that the Pale Suits visited, the gamelan sang to me, and it sang from a shanty town on the edge of the

great city of Djakarta, the music of its gongs shimmering and
dancing in the Javanese dusk. Behind the knot of musicians the
shanty town stretched away until it disappeared in the haze of
cooking fires. The music of the ensemble was very solemn; it
spoke of the land the people had struggled for and lost, of their
flight to the city, and of the new poverty they had found there.
The steady chime of the gongs reached into the corners of the
furthest houses, so that it seemed in the end that the entire
shanty town echoed with sadness for a time when better things
had been promised, and the promises had come to nothing. As
night fell, the music faded into silence, and I saw a small boy,
asleep on the dirt floor of a hut, clutching in his arms a perfectly
made model of the great gongs my grandfather had spoken of.
Although he was fast asleep, he held the gong so tightly to his
chest that it was possible to believe it was his only possession in
the world. But now that the gamelan had ceased, the shanty
town was slipping into shadow, and before long I was back in
the gloom of the hall, waiting again for our visitors to emerge,
the instruments lifeless shapes around me.

I no longer had the courage to visit my grandfather in his
room, so I went out and waited for him by the orchard.
Eventually he came across the lawn, moving like a blind man,
groping his way to his chair beneath the trees. I watched as he
tried to speak, his tongue lolling between thickened lips, and I
knew then that if his treatment continued in this way it would
eventually silence him altogether. I never thought of discussing
any of this with my mother. For some years now she had been
so detached that her presence in the house seemed almost
accidental. We did not discuss the Pale Suits and my grandfather's treatment because we did not discuss anything of
importance. It seemed that some part of her had become too
fragile to exist in the world of the Pale Suits, so that she had
retreated to the sanctuary of her bedroom, a room whose only
concrete reality for me was as the source of the mysterious
scents and beautiful clothes she wore.

Then something happened which changed the course of the
summer. One evening I looked from my window and saw a
glow on the horizon, a glow which flared gradually brighter
until it lit up a great section of the central city. At one point I
thought I heard the distant sound of explosions. It was nearly
dawn before the glow subsided to a dull red. The next day there
was increased activity on the road outside, with the long cars of

the Pale Suits travelling faster and in greater numbers than I had ever seen. In mid-afternoon there was almost an accident, when a driver approached our bend too fast and had to struggle to keep his vehicle under control. I saw a momentary look of fear on the face of the Pale Suit at the wheel, a look that stayed with me for long afterwards. It had never occurred to me that Pale Suits might be able to experience fear. The activity on the road outside continued into the next day, which was a treatment day for my grandfather, and the two of us sat in the orchard and listened to the steady sound of the passing vehicles. My grandfather was slumped in his chair, watching the drive in silence. Even the most halting reminiscence now seemed beyond him. Flies from the orchard settled on his face and arms and he did not seem to have the strength to wave them away. The hot afternoon stretched out for an age, and to pass the time I counted the vehicles as they took the corner. By dusk I had counted a hundred and forty-two and yet the Pale Suits had still not arrived, so at last we went inside to eat. There was a feeling of unreality about the meal that night, I could not recall the Pale Suits having ever missed a treatment day before.

This feeling continued into the rest of the week as the Pale Suits still failed to call. Outside the vehicles came and went on the road, sometimes alone, sometimes in great convoys, but none of them pulled up in the drive, and by the end of the following week the Pale Suits had missed five treatment days in all. By now I had begun to notice small changes in my grandfather. He moved among the trees in the orchard more freely, his shoulders were straighter and he no longer trailed the faint smell of urine that once had followed him about the house.

Before long his reminiscences began again, and now they were a little easier to follow. Tales that had once baffled me with their shifting locations and broken plots started to hang together, as though a fragile thread had begun to run among the scattered pieces of his memory. Some of his stories stirred in me a strange feeling of recognition, as though I had heard them before but when too young to remember or to properly understand. He spoke of his voyages among the endless atoll chains of Micronesia; he told me of the time he had contracted a rare strain of malaria in the Mariana Islands and of being paralysed by village liquor in Guam. The liquor had been drunk at a celebration to mark his mastery of the rare stomach bow after months of apprenticeship to the leading musician on the island.

He had lain in a coma for ten days, and on coming to, had been presented with one of the oldest bows on the island, cut from hibiscus wood and strung with finest pineapple fibre. Through some special reasoning that was never explained to him, his coma had been taken as a sign of exceptional suitability for the instrument.

My grandfather told his stories with a new vigour now. There was no stopping him once he had begun on a tale, as though the long months of his treatment had diverted his memories into a dammed lake of the imagination, and the obstruction that had been holding them back had now been cleared away. Instruments which had lain in dusty corners of the house for years and whose origins had been a mystery to me became suddenly recognisable – I identified the stomach bow from Guam at once. The instrument hung in one of the unused rooms, a length of curved wood with a split gourd half-way down its length. My grandfather explained that the gourd was placed against the musician's stomach to amplify the vibrations of the fibre string. From his tales I also identified a shawm from Guatemala, a nose flute from Truk and a log drum from the Philippines.

We would sit in the orchard until after dusk, the trees turning to dim shapes around us, the line of distant mountains catching the last of the light, as my grandfather exercised his returning memory and the fruit flies gathered in clouds above our heads.

It was very peaceful there in the orchard, the vehicles on the road outside were another world away, and I began to believe that the Pale Suits had bypassed us, that we no longer had any place in their scheme of things. We had come to a silent agreement not to discuss this, however, for fear that we might alter some delicate balance of invisible forces that was keeping them away.

My mother was unaffected by the absence of the Pale Suits. She came and went in the house in the way that she had always done, appearing in the morning and for meals and retiring to her room for the rest of the day. The house, however, had changed. The windows now let in more light, the dust on the floor did not seem so thick, and the doorways of the unused rooms no longer gaped like mouths onto the hallway. The house was breathing again. I could sense the sweeter air moving among the rooms, and although the instruments were no longer singing to me, they rested more easily in their corners and on their shelves. I felt sometimes that the instruments were beginning to replace my sisters and my father, and I thought of them as more real in some ways than those distant members of my family who had gone away to the mountains so many years before.

In the orchard my grandfather's pomegranates had reached their full maturity, and the branches of the trees bent almost to the ground with the weight of the fruit. The day had come to taste the first of the fruit and we decided to hold a small celebration to mark the occasion. We set up a table under the trees and spread it with a white cloth. My grandfather laid out two plates and a cutting board, and I hunted through the drawers until I found the sharpest knife in the kitchen. We knew which of the pomegranates we would choose; we had been watching it for weeks. It hung on a tree near the bottom of the orchard, perfectly formed and with an unmarked skin of deep crimson. My grandfather took the fruit from the tree, placed it in the middle of the cutting board, and we sat down facing each other across the table. We had agreed that I would carve the pomegranate and he would be the first to taste its flesh. When I cut into the fruit I thought that I had never seen a brighter splash of red, and the juice ran in rivulets across the board and stained the white of the table-cloth. My grandfather lifted the pomegranate to his mouth and bit into the flesh, his hands trembling a little as they always did when he ate. I was watching the pleasure spread across his face, when a movement in the direction of the house caught my eye. At the edge of the orchard, standing very still and watching us intently, was a Pale Suit. My grandfather was so engrossed in the fruit that he did not see the expression on my face, he went on eating the pomegranate until he had finished it, while I sat there across the table from him, unable to take my eyes from the stain of the juice on the white table-cloth.

When they had gone inside with my grandfather, I dragged the table around the house and placed it under the windows of the front room. By standing on the table I could reach the level of the window, and although the curtains were drawn, I found that by positioning the table carefully I was able to see a part of the room. At first I could not pick out any details, but as my eyes began to adjust I made out my grandfather's feet on the end of the bed, shoeless and still. Beyond his feet something winked in the gloom of the room, and after a while I realised that it was the light catching the turning reels of a tape machine. I stood there, mesmerised by the reels, my face against the window, and I might still have been there when the curtains were thrown back, if a pale shape had not moved between the machine and the window and broken into my trance.

I carried the table back to the orchard, and set out the cloth and plates as we had left them. Then I went inside to where the stomach bow hung on the wall. I concentrated on the instrument, listening for the hum of its fibre string. Nothing disturbed the quiet of the room. I tried again, straining into the silence, searching for the echo of the distant atolls, and knowing now that it was more important than ever to communicate with the instruments. But the bow would not sing to me; it remained mute and still on its hook on the wall, and I realised then that in my weeks away from the instruments I had lost my old intimacy with them, and I did not know how I was going to close the gap that now separated us. I thought of the pale shapes moving in the gloom, of the turning reels of the tape machine, of the other, unseen contents of the aluminium case that our visitors always brought with them. And I thought about the change that had come over them while they had been away. The Pale Suits had been impassive before; they had come and gone without showing any sign of emotion in their work. But there was something different about them now, a new tension, as though a deep anger lay behind their bland faces. Our visitors were in the front room for longer than I could ever recall, and eventually, exhausted by the knowledge of their return and by my attempts to rouse the instruments, I fell asleep on the floor of the unused room. Much later I seemed to hear the sound of my mother calling, and because she was calling something that was strange to me I could not decide whether I was dreaming. I lay still, and after a long pause I heard her voice again and realised that I was awake and that she was calling to my grandfather in the orchard. I got up and went outside to where the evening light had begun to illuminate the back garden. When I saw the orchard I stopped. Not a single pomegranate remained on the trees. In the middle of the orchard, swaying slightly on his feet, was my grandfather, and around him in all directions lay the remains of the crop of pomegranates. In his hands he held a heavy stick, and his shoes were crusted and stained from trampling the fruit as they lay on the ground. He was squinting into the trees, inspecting each in turn to make sure that he had not missed any of the fruit, and then he threw down the stick and walked past me towards the drive. He stumbled a little, regained his balance and went off down the drive like a blind man, leaving behind him in the gravel a trail of seeds and red pulp. I saw my mother, pale and motionless, watching us from the porch. She seemed to be looking past the wreckage of the orchard to the mountains beyond, and I knew then that she was thinking of the others, but I could not tell from her face whether she believed we would ever see them again. Then she turned and went back into the house. My grandfather was nearly at the road now and I ran after him down the drive. Although the traffic had fallen off a little in recent days, the road was busy, and the great vehicles of the Pale Suits still came and went at speed. I had almost reached the bottom of the drive when my grandfather crossed the pavement and went out onto the road. A vehicle that had just rounded the corner made a wide arc to avoid him, its horn blaring and its tyres crabbing on the asphalt. My grandfather followed it with vacant eyes as it pulled to a halt further down the road. The driver looked back at us through his rear window. By now I had my grandfather by the elbow and was leading him to the pavement. I raised an arm to the driver in the hope that he would drive on. As I led my grandfather back up the drive, I heard the vehicle pulling away into the stream of traffic. Back at the house my grandfather sat in the kitchen looking into space. He did not move or speak for several hours, and eventually I had to lead him like a sleep-walker to his bed.

As though making up for lost time the Pale Suits returned the next day and on this occasion they brought their vehicle to the top of the drive. When they got out I saw why. On the back seat, in place of the usual case, there was a much larger case made of the same bright aluminium and heavy enough to need both of the men to lift it. They were too concerned with getting the case into the house to notice the condition of the orchard. They carried the case down the passage and past the gamelan to the front room, and as they did so I imagined I heard the low chime of a gong, as though the instrument had been brushed in passing. My grandfather sat in the kitchen, watching the Pale Suits come and go, his blue eyes sharp and feverish. When the front room was ready the Pale Suits came into the kitchen and waited for my grandfather to get up. He remained in his chair, his arms limp before him on the table. The three of them seemed to be there an age, the men standing silent by the door and my grandfather motionless in his chair.

At last he got to his feet and went out into the hall, and I knew then that his resistance was over, that his last defence lay in the wreckage of the orchard and that the Pale Suits would now be able to do with him what they wished. When the door to the front room had closed behind them the house became very quiet and I tasted the stale air moving once more through the unused rooms, ebbing and flowing among the inert instruments. Then from the hallway I heard the chime of the gamelan, and as I listened it came once more, a low echo on the dead air. The instruments were waking again, and they had not waited for me to try to reach them first. The chime of the gamelan was solemn and regular now, welling up through the house like a heartbeat, until I could feel it through the soles of my feet and sense its heavy pulse in the pit of my belly. I saw again the shanty towns of Djakarta, the smoke haze low over the huts, and my grandfather sitting cross-legged in the circle of gamelan players; and then through the sound of the gamelan like a sharpened blade came the pure tone of the lute, singing from the deserts of Chile, telling of the ancient music that anchored the past of the people against the shifting sands of the desert. And now other instruments were waking and crowding in on the lute; I heard the sigh of the Guatemalan shawm and the rapid beat of the Filipino log drum. Instruments that had never sung before were breaking their years of silence, emerging from their dusty corners of the house for the first time in order to jostle for place in a chaotic rising choir. The air around me was alive with rhythms that broke in on other rhythms, with melodies that surfaced briefly before being drowned by the surge of some new voice joining the chorus, as instruments struggled to find their true voices after years of disuse. Slowly the milling sounds began to take on some order, the instruments were beginning to complement each other, as though fumbling their way towards a common voice. And then they began to sing in concert, sometimes one taking the lead, sometimes another. They sang of the howl of the typhoon in the tin roofs of the great shanty towns of the East, of the blinding rains and steaming heat; they sang of the harsh lives of the shanty town dwellers and of the peasant farmers on their meagre plots of land. I heard then of the hopes of the people for another life, of their struggle to make a new, better order from the old ... and suddenly the music of the instruments grew dark and discordant, and the gamelan sang of blood on the grass of the teak forests of Java, the lute spoke of burning huts in the Chilean deserts, and the drum beat out the rap of midnight fists on the doors of Filipino slums.

And like shadows appearing in the cities and in the country-side, I saw men in pale clothing who emerged from the dusk, who stood on street corners and listened in market-places, who went quietly among the people with their soft, sing-song voices, watching and waiting, and who moved when they were ready with deadly swiftness to still the struggles of the poor. I knew then as the dark chords of the music swirled around me that my grandfather had been touched by these things, that his life of travel among the peoples of the Pacific, the secrets he had learnt from them, the music he loved and its sacred place at the heart of their cultures – all this had eventually led him to the dim front room of his own house, where the pale figures of our visitors attended him on a urine-soaked bed, while a lifetime's knowledge slipped through his mind like water through sand.

At that moment the chorus of instruments stopped abruptly and I heard the door of the front room burst open and the sound of feet in the hall. The Pale Suits stood in the doorway, looking about them at the silent instruments. One of the men wore gloves of pale rubber that came half-way up to his elbows. The Pale Suit with the gloves went over to the stomach bow and gently plucked its fibre string. The instrument gave out a low, dull sound, as though it had hung there untuned and unplayed for twenty years. He listened as the note faded into the corners of the room, watching me closely as he did so. 'A young musician,' he said. 'Following in the footsteps of his grand-father.' The Pale Suit walked among the instruments, sometimes running a gloved finger across a dusty body or plucking a slack string. When he had finished his inspection he stood once more in the doorway with the other man, gazing thoughtfully around the room. Then he turned and the two of them went back down the hall to the front room.

Later I sat in the chair at the edge of the ruined orchard and watched the Pale Suits load the instruments into their vehicle. First they packed the gamelan, after dismantling it into its various pieces, and then added the stomach bow, the lute, and the Filipino log drum. When they had stripped the house of the last of its instruments they climbed into the vehicle, backed slowly down the drive and moved off in the direction of the city.

I set off for the mountains that night; travelling only by darkness and avoiding the roads, I estimated that it would take me ten days to reach them. I did not know how I would find my sisters and my father when I got there, or even whether they were still alive, but I knew that I could not stay to watch the final decline of the house. I saw it then as the Pale Suits would eventually leave it, gutted and open to the weather. I saw the wind lifting the iron of the roof, the rain beating through open windows onto the floor ... I saw my grandfather wandering through its empty rooms and I saw him going out to sit by a blackened orchard overgrown with weeds, freed at last of the intolerable burden of his memories.

Githa Hariharan

from THE GHOSTS OF VASU MASTER

Mangala's Journeys

Once, when the four of us – Mangala, Vishnu, Venu and I,
made one of our rare trips away from Elipettai, we went to the
seaside a little outside Madras. We never saw the crowded
Marina that we had heard so much about: but this quiet strip of
beach away from the heart of the city drew us day after day.

The boys, innocent of travel, landlocked in dusty Elipettai,
had of course seen nothing like it. Even Mangala suddenly
seemed different: more receptive, open to the possibility of
change. It was as if an entire week of breathing damp, salty air;
the freedom from routine and the freedom of muddy clothes;
the importance of finding shells intact; and above all, the cool,
mysterious secret of the waves, drew Mangala out of herself;
allowed her to briefly shed her customary reticence.

The boys and I held hands and waded into the sea, just far
enough for little Venu to be submerged up to his chest. Vishnu
and he shrieked with delighted fright every time a large wave
came billowing forward, crashed, and knocked us under.

Mangala did not come into the water with us. She walked

The Ghosts of Vasu Master is about a retired schoolmaster in a small Indian
town. Out of the classroom after forty years, reduced to the teacher of one child
– who does not speak – Vasu Master struggles to teach, and heal, both the child
and himself. As part of this process of self-discovery, Vasu reconstructs the lives
of the women in his life, all of them now, in one sense or the other, ghosts. In
this extract, Vasu meets his dead wife, Mangala; her friend and sewing teacher,
Jameela; and a fisherwoman, Eliamma. Their intertwined stories make a distinct
strand in Vasu's (and the novel's) weaving together of memory, fantasy and self-
knowledge.

along the seashore, looking for shells, or stray evidence of the secret sandy life of crustaceans – all kinds of odd things to add to the children's collection. She poked at the sand with a twig, sending a host of startled and indignant crabs scurrying about. But most of the time she sat on the sand, at a distance from the shoreline where she could see us; though it was not our childish splashing that she looked at, but some remote point in the distance where sea melted into sky.

As she fed the boys at night, Venu half asleep, leaning against her side so that she had to keep nudging him awake, Vishnu asked her: Amma, why don't you come into the water with us? Can't you swim?

I could, Mangala told him. I used to swim in the village pond till I was nine or ten. But now – I don't know – can you forget swimming?

My wife and sons looked toward me for an opinion. But I didn't know either, and Vishnu said with something like triumph: Amma can't swim. Amma can't cycle – And before he could go on with his list, Venu suddenly woke up and interrupted him.

But she has seen ghosts and we haven't.

Vishnu, as Venu had expected, was immediately squashed. Both of them considered Mangala a ghost-expert. She knew hundreds of ghost stories, though it was not always easy to make her part with one. When she gave away one of these stories, it was an unexpected, exotic gift. Part of the gift was the air about her when she spoke of ghosts, an air which told us that she knew what she was talking about; that she was on familiar, even intimate terms with her ethereal heroes and heroines.

So Vishnu, having forgotten about swimming altogether, now coaxed Mangala: Amma, tell us a true ghost story. A real one.

No, interrupted Venu, indignant. (He had introduced the subject after all.) Tell us a very very strange ghost story.

Let's see, said Mangala, unruffled as ever. A story that's true and strange?

Eliamma Goes Fishing

The important thing to remember about ghosts, Mangala began, is that they were not always like that: souls with no bodies; bodies with no matter, or life as we know it.

So when I first saw Eliamma at her usual waiting-post, the seashore lit by a harvest moon, she was not a ghost but a woman with a very real body. She was in fact beautiful, with thick, long hair and tapering, fish-shaped eyes. She wore an old but spotless white mundu, and her choli was a deep midnight blue.

She lived in the old fishing village by the sea, and was brought up to be a fisherwoman like the rest of her kind. But something set her apart from the other villagers. It could have been her remote, disturbing sort of beauty – her eyes always intent, as if straining to see something at a great distance: something as yet unknown, hidden in the depths of the waters mid-sea.

Eliamma did her share of fisherwomen's work: she made herself useful mending nets, cleaning fish, drying them. She went to church with the other young women. But she did not seem to have either family or friends. The story was that she had many admirers and could have married any of the young fishermen; but she continued to live alone in her hut, and to wander by the seashore at odd hours of the night. People said they had never seen her smile. They said she had a secret: that she was in love, though no one knew who the beloved was.

Eliamma walked alone by the sea night after night. She looked out into the watery horizon with longing. She yearned to go far beyond the distance she could swim. She wanted to be in the centre of the expanse she saw, in a womb held in place by the ocean's ancient secrets.

As a girl she had thought she could do this by persuading the fishermen to take her with them when they set out on the open sea. She knew now that this would never happen; they would only laugh at her and tease her as they had then, or call her mad.

On the nights when the fishermen set out in their long, narrow boats which made trembling arrow-like shadows on the water, she hid herself, but she watched them till the dark spots were swallowed up by the night sea.

One night, Eliamma was sitting behind an old boat that was no longer sea-worthy. It was grounded high up on the sand near the two guardians of the village, a man and a woman with fearsome faces. Their bodies were plastered white except for the eyes which were painted a fixed, staring black. Their blood-red mouths were stretched wide open so that their tongues hung out as far as they could. Both figures were seated on horse-like creatures; both faced the sea with their grim, forbidding faces, as if daring the waters to intrude beyond their allotted territory.

Eliamma looked at them for a while; then she turned her face to its usual position, and looked out to the sea like the guardians. She fell asleep.

When she woke up, everything around her was dim and unfamiliar. Then she remembered where she was; she licked her lips and felt salt on her tongue. The sea nearby sounded choppy and rough. Eliamma suddenly scrambled to her feet, wondering if a freak storm was about to break.

Then she saw the stranger. He stood only a few feet away, so she couldn't believe she had not seen him right away.

Her first thought was escape. In her moment of panic, she looked into the stranger's face and was about to make a flurried sign of the cross. She also turned around to run, but didn't. She made herself look at him again. He was tall, thin; his bones jutted out in sharp angles so that he looked skeletal in the moonlight. Though he did not seem young, the face was smooth; and it wore a sweet, gentle expression as if it belonged to a kind, benevolent uncle.

In a sudden flash of lightning, she also saw his eyes. There was nothing frightening about them either. They were as limpid as hers; they seemed in fact to be pleading with her.

Eliamma suspected that their meeting was no accident. Though he had not yet said a word to her, she felt the stranger had sought her out; to give her a very special, unusual gift.

Who are you? she asked him. What do you want?

He looked at her steadily.

Then he suddenly whispered, And you, Eliamma, what do you want? Do you still want to travel across the ocean?

She was so amazed that he knew her name and her secret – all of her it seemed – that she immediately said, Yes.

I can help you, he told her. I can help you go out to sea in the fishing boats.

She felt a sharp pang of disappointment. I've tried that years ago, she said impatiently. They won't let me.

But they could see you then. What if they don't know you are with them?

He had her attention again. Tell me what to do, she said. I'll do anything.

When he heard these words, his face relaxed; he was almost smiling.

I have – ah – a special quality, he told her. I am invisible. You see me now, but that is a brief illusion, given to my kind once every thirty years.

Can you make me invisible? asked Eliamma. (She could see it was the only way she would ever get a place on a fishing boat.)

Yes, he replied, for as long as you like. I will take care of your visible body till then – and wait for you.

Eliamma was as impatient as he was. She couldn't be bothered with details till she had tried it out. So they went round the plaster guardians: he round the female twice; she round the male thrice. And Eliamma felt herself being lifted out of her body till she was as light and insubstantial as air, and as invisible.

As she raced down the shore to stow herself in a boat that would leave the morning after, she turned around once. She saw the body she had left behind walking away.

Hey you, she called out. She could not hear her voice – she heard only the roar of the waves – but he (or the body) turned around.

What do I do when I want to go back to my body? she called out.

Look for me on the seashore. You'll find me after a month near the old boat, he said to the empty air and hurried away.

For a week or two, Eliamma was happier than she had ever been. The sea was sometimes the mother she had not known: the quiet rhythmic beating of the waves against the boat lulled her to a safe, watery place; a restful sleep. Sometimes the sea was different: it was awesome, demanding, given to unpredictable swings of mood. She loved this face too. She loved the excitement of her body balancing precariously in a fragile boat against the rage and passion of the sea.

She felt no hunger or thirst like the fishermen, so she felt no desire to go back to land. She saw a tiny rocky island on the high sea and she lifted herself off the boat like a wisp of breeze.

On her rock, surrounded by the sea, Eliamma lost count of time. She saw the fishermen come and go, and once she heard their voices over the water, speaking in hushed, reverent tones of her rock. They called it the guardian of the mid-ocean.

Many sunrises and sunsets later, Eliamma drifted into one of these boats and went back to the shore in search of the stranger. There was, she had found, a catch to being invisible. Everything she touched sickened, froze, died, or became invisible to everybody but her. If she scooped out fish from the sea to load a poor fisherman's boat, the fish lay in the boat, unseen, till it began to rot. Every day she scooped out invisible handfuls of rotting fish from boats, or off her rocky island, and threw them back into the sea. Green and brown tentacles of seaweed, barnacles, turtles, jellyfish – everything fell apart if she touched it.

Then she knew why the stranger had been so generous, so quick to part with his riches; to be completely invisible was to be lonely in a way the living did not know.

Eliamma did not find him anywhere on the shore. Though she haunted the old boat, the twin guardians with the gruesome painted faces, she saw no one who resembled the stranger; or her earlier, live self.

So Eliamma waits, said Mangala to our two wide-eyed sons. She waits and waits, a patient ghost, for the day she will find someone who sees her briefly. Someone who will willingly accept her freakish gift.

Begum Three-in-One

When I remembered Eliamma's voyage, I saw the familiar watery landscape that deepened as it flowed toward the horizon. Eliamma was as insubstantial as a puff of air; her natural habitat mid-ocean, a mere speck to the naked eye. I knew she was part of the vista before me only because I saw a less obscure womanly figure on the shoreline.

As I gazed at the setting my feminine ghosts were partial to, the scene took on a silken appearance – a shimmer in the gloss or wave, or the sheer quality of skin and sari; a grainy knot of thread in the velvety texture of sky and sand. I was looking at the last canvas Jameela had embroidered on Mangala's behalf: a hazy seascape in which all was ambiguous movement, suggestive of mysterious possibility. I knew immediately that nothing tangible would survive here; no recognisable creature of flesh and blood.

Eliamma, Mangala and Jameela were, in my mind at least, ineluctably linked, always hand in hand. But though one had gone ahead of the other, both Eliamma and Mangala were receding ghosts. Their stories and Jameela's, for all their common motifs, were different.

Jameela was no spirit. Her full body was warm and alive under her ineffectual burqa. Though she was lost to me, Jameela,

I was sure, was not lost to life. She would survive. Even as I thought this, a voice I dimly recognised as mine cried aloud. Where are you? Why are you hiding? And I saw in the lustrous panorama before me a creation of Jameela's enchanted loom – her unspoken reply, her very own story.

Jameela said to me: There were three caterpillars who crawled out of their eggs one by one. They looked at each other and liked what they saw, so the eldest, Ammukutty, said to the younger caterpillars: Nanikutty, Ummikutty, let's be friends and live on this tree always. Nanikutty and Ummikutty agreed, and without wasting time on further discussion the three immediately began to chomp leaves in sisterly togetherness.

They ate and ate and grew several furry bulges each. A week or two later, they suddenly stopped; one, then the next, and their friendly munching noise gave way to a companionable silence. Then Ammukutty split the baby skin that had got too tight for her, exposing a vibrant blue skin underneath: the kind you might imagine on a deep-sea creature. She taught Nanikutty how to shed her skin and turn the fresh colour of fields, using all the possible shades of green: and Nanikutty in turn taught young Ummikutty to shut her eyes and wriggle gently out of her old skin, to emerge a glorious, sunny orange.

Now that the three sisters had passed their first test with flying colours, they went back to their regular business of chomping leaves. But this time they combined chewing with a few other simple pleasures. They found, for instance, two little knobs on their heads which they could use like antennae, to learn about the world around and beyond their tree-home. And they discovered the spinnerets on their heads too: from these they could put out long, slim threads of silk.

They put this talent to all sorts of uses: if they fell from a branch or leaf, they spun threads to drop gently to earth. If they wanted to return, they climbed these same threads. And as for fun and games! They walked on trails of silk to their hearts' content. They glided from one leaf to another by spinning bridges: they played Catch the Caterpillar's Tail or Push Off the Leaf for hours with great shrieks of glee.

Once Ammukutty, Nanikutty and Ummikutty had shed skins a second and a third and a fourth time, they began, like the eager young things they were, to talk among themselves: of what

they would see and do once they were through with the childish
pleasure of stuffing themselves. They took turns describing their
futures. This they did by twisting their silk threads into all kinds
of fantastic shapes, so that they not only heard each other's
words but saw before them, in a series of swiftly changing
pictures, their varied dreams. They learnt designs and new
stitches from each other. By the time they were ready to sleep in
the three gray bags they planned to sew for themselves, they had
a common fund of patterns, a rich mingling of dreams.

One by one they stopped eating. Then Ammukutty began to
move her head slowly, back and forth in a sensuous dance; the
other two followed. Ammukutty threw out one thread after
another, swinging her head to make the figure eight. Soon all
three sisters were caught in this rapturous, serpentine movement.
They danced faster and faster, spun more and more thread in
dizzy circles for three whole days.

Exhausted, they shrank neatly into the safety of their cocoons
and rested. They slept a sound sleep, not doubting that they
would meet each other again as official, full-fledged lady moths.

They were so fast asleep that they did not hear voices below
their tree. The voices came from three travelling brothers – well-
known in their hometown not only for their cleverness, but also
because they were identical triplets: Chief Triplet, Middle Triplet
and Third Triplet.

Chief, a sharp-eyed one, looked up at the sky to see if it was
clear enough for their journey home. It was, but his eyes also
took in something else: hanging from a twig above, three bags
of gray silk so fine that they shimmered like glass when the sun
shone on them.

Chief lost no time telling his brothers about the luscious
silkworms he had seen. All three wanted a bag of threads each;
they could already see the silk in their minds, its soft lustre and
beautiful colours. Chief told them: If there's a lot of thread, we
can take it back home and get rich. If there isn't, there will be
enough to get us a silken robe or two; we can swagger about
town like princes.

Chief quickly added, It's my turn first. Middle and Third
respectfully moved aside to watch him. Chief was a young man
of great foresight. So he didn't rush up the tree right away as
the others had expected. Instead he set about getting things
ready. He pulled out a saucepan from his travelling bag and
went in search of a spring. When he had filled it with water, he

set fire to a pile of broken branches. He placed the saucepan on the fire when it was good and strong. Soon the water was bubbling, sending up spiral clouds of steam.

Chief rubbed his hands together and said, Now! He climbed up the tree like an agile monkey and plucked Ammukutty off the twig with one quick grab. Ammukutty shrieked as he slipped down the tree-trunk with her. He didn't hear her, not having conversed with hibernating caterpillars before. But Nanikutty and Ummikutty heard their sister, though they couldn't do a thing to help because it was too soon for them to open up their bags. So they heard and suffered silently. Once Ammukutty's screams grew faint, they had to go back to their dreaming; except this time, they wove in, with fine silken knots, the life and dreams of Ammukutty.

Middle and Third watched their brother come down with an almost ripe cocoon. Without a moment's doubt, Chief dropped Ammukutty into the water bubbling on the fire. The cocoon bobbed up and down like a lost boat; a vulnerable island on a stormy sea. When Ammukutty was cooked to a pinkish gray tube of meat, the air was filled with the foul stench of rotting fish. Middle and Third held their noses in disgust. But Chief wrapped a thick cloth around his hand and unwound the shining threads of the empty cocoon. He pulled the thread gently, unravelled it with all his cleverness, till he had yards and yards of fresh silk in his bag. It smelt awful, but that didn't bother him; silken robes and princely titles didn't come without raising a bit of a stink.

Now it was Middle's turn. He was a mild, fearful sort. He wanted things all right, but he didn't feel too happy about the grabbing involved. He and Third said goodbye to Chief (who was in a hurry to get home), and Middle sat down to think. He talked to Third; he talked to himself; sometimes, when terribly mixed up, he even tried talking to the sleeping Nanikutty who had fallen to his lot. Finally Third, tired of all this wishy-washy self-examination, snapped at him: We're running out of time! Go up and do what you have to like a man!

Middle had to swallow all his excuses, doubts and questions, and climb the tree. It took him a while (as everything did) and by the time he reached the branch closest to the twig he wanted, Nanikutty was almost emerging from her chrysalis. Middle saw (with relief and self-loathing) that he was a little too late: she had already grown wings, though they were still moist and stuck to her sides. He picked her bag off the twig tenderly so that she would not scream as Ammukutty had. (But Ummikutty, though puzzled by the silence, knew what was going on.)

Middle took Nanikutty down, bag and stuck wings and all, and put her into a box made of fine, porous paper. He took the box home, where Nanikutty slowly got used to life in a paper box. She knew would never see Ummikutty again; never unfold her wings and test them out. But she laid the eggs a well-brought up lady moth should, all the time spinning those old dreams in her head, round and round herself like a warm, safe shroud.

And Ummikutty? How did she fare with Third Triplet? The poor fellow had waited so long, what with Chief's elaborate preparation for the kill and Middle's procrastination, that by the time Third got to climb the tree, Ummikutty was out of her cocoon. When he neared the twig, she opened her wings and flew away. Third was left with only a husk. He took it anyway, as consolation prize.

So of the three sisters, only Ummikutty was left on the tree, and she was understandably nervous about her safety. Her sisters' dreams had also left her with some peculiar marks. Her wings, unlike those of the other lady moths she had seen flying around at night, grew more and more flashy. Her antennae had become hyper-sensitive; and she had not yet lost her ability to produce line after line of fine silk, or weave them into fantastic shapes.

Ummikutty, aware of the dangers around her, looked for a hiding place. Every time she heard a voice below the trees, she remembered the Triplets and she flew to the bag she had made for herself, a cocoon with a difference. She hid in the shapeless, camouflaging sack she had neatly stitched together with large green leaves.

Jameela said to me: Ummikutty, as far as I know, is still in hiding somewhere in the forest, weaving on her old spinning loom. Year in and year out, she designs a tapestry full of meaning; but whatever she weaves is also ever-dissolving. If you saw her creations, the colours and shapes she uses, you would understand why she is no longer called Ummikutty; why she has grown into Begum Three-in One. The stories she spins, you see, are not all her own, and not always easy to unravel; because all of them weave in, with the finest of silk threads, the ghosts of her lost sisters.

Adib Khan

RAINBOW VOICES

In the eerie light between dawn and morning there are such wondrous pleasures to be stolen. Moments of blinding intimation beyond the logic of understanding. In the swirling tunnel the flute of levitation sounds clearly like the clinking of breaking glass. The mystery of desire is in the feeling of touching the peaks of self. And yet . . . and yet we come away empty-handed with the bare remnants of memory.

What a night!

Eyes feasted. Eager hands and a salivating mouth awed by the splendour of possibilities. A ride over a golden brown landscape. Explorers went their separate ways to confront the riddle of the universe. Glimpsed richness of kings for those who cared to seek.

What is the mystery of darkness you hide inside? Tell me.

Her legs quivered and the slabs of thighs gave way like noiseless doors, opening to an altar deep inside a hidden chamber. Among the dew-kissed tendrils lay protrusions of livid flesh quivering in fearful protest. A brief journey accompanied by the noise of tom-toms celebrating the ritual of creation.

The dream-laden ship gathered its treasures and departed without warning, chased away by the fear of betrayal. I think of the garden and a night of thousand Eves with identical faces, tossing in the tide of my lust.

Vamana (in Hindu mythology, Vamana, the dwarf, is one of the incarnations of Visnu) is a very ugly, bisexual, story-telling dwarf. He works in Delhi with a group of thieves who are controlled by an underworld character, Barey Bhai (Big Brother). His story is narrated while he is in prison for assault, theft, and setting fire to the house of a property developer. This is an extract from a novel-in-progress.

Meena ... Meena ... Ah, the imperfection of memory. It is an unreliable walkway between dreams and desires. All that remains is a whiff of crushed jasmine wafting from the other side of the locked door.

So here I am, under a young and flawless sky without the speckles of hopeful vultures. Slowly the dome begins to burn with a feverish intensity. Bare earth. Distances and sleepy trees. Morning will soon stir into a cacophony of voices. I must hide . . .

What do you hear inside?

Nothing.

Nothing?

The silence of Paradise.

And who lives in this Paradise?

Broken people. Charred dreams.

Can you explain that?

It's not of this world.

The guard whistles mindlessly, his fingers caressing the trigger of the rifle he carries. The morning's innocence has already faded. There's the doleful sound of the prison's bell.

I have long hours in the company of daylight ghosts.

He is staring at me. A barked command. Mounds of broken bricks have to be pounded into smaller pieces.

I look around. There is nowhere to go. Escape is a remote possibility beyond my courage.

Others will be arriving today.

You will have company in your cell.

I would rather be by myself.

Prisons cannot afford such luxuries.

The thud of the hammer cracks the silence.

A flutter of fearful flight.

The hammer descends again. And again . . .

In a deep cave, somewhere beyond the grove, a flame flickers. It's time . . . What is more precious? The things we see or what we imagine? Which is more lasting? How shall I measure the worth of remembrances? Memory is the mind's storyteller. It gurgles and splutters, forever awake.

Barey, you should have more sense!

Baji?

You should have chosen with more care! What have you sent me? Ay larka! How long does it take you to fetch me a tumbler of water? Hai kismet! When I ask him to do something, he blinks and grins! How coarse are his hands! He refuses to wash.

*His breath is sour and his stories . . . Ugly! Ugly! He enjoys
destroying all that I imagine to be beautiful!*

If you wish I can . . .

*No. It's too late. Repulsive as he is, he is one of us. A freak.
An accident. A hellish creature transported to this life by
mistake. His body is the Devil's work. His mind is an inferno.
He spends his hours burning in his own fire. See how he grins.
He shelters demons inside him . . .*

Harsh words, but without malice. Baji was utterly confounded
by my extraordinary incompetence in domestic chores. How
was I to explain that I was handcuffed to my imagination? Had
someone even whispered that dreaming was a self-destructive
vocation, I might have disengaged myself from the playful
shadows of a weeping moon and emerged as a responsible being.
The mind is an uncharted land, a habitat for the improbable
and the fantastic. The sordid and the perverse. Anything is
possible. It hums with sounds and teems with images. Light and
shade. Elusive faces. Monsters and bhoots. It is my mission to
describe them and give them substance by encapsulating them
in words. Words! And what are words but sharp knives that
create entrances into dimly perceived worlds? Noises and scrib-
bles that give shape and colour to the terrifying flux of chaos.
Deep inside, there are no norms or conventions. Nothing
surprises. An abode without walls or laws. A self-renewing life
without the blight of time. It is a kind of floating. An endless
dance to a favourite tune which keeps repeating itself. Here
there is no need for pretensions of sanity or false modesty. The
streets are crowded with naked people who do not know how
to hide their thoughts. Among them I am a hero. A judge. A
vigilant God wary of intruding Adams. It is a haven never to be
surrendered to the insidious forces of cause and effect.

I am a creator of life. Meanings. Of seeds that germinate and
flame into the trees of possibilities. I do not seek to shape
perfection. My mind is like Ali Baba's cave. Open Sesame!
Behold! A galaxy of illusions. The birth of ideas and words.
Collapsing universes. Even as I create, lives end. I crack open
the earth and lacerate it with crevices. The world is smeared
with shadows. Ships sink and mountains dissolve. The aged fuck
to celebrate the shedding of beauty. The young – so chaste and
cold. Women cry. Children shiver. The howl of wolves and the
laughter of demons are stored in the shell of memory.

It's all inside. All inside. I must play the buffoon to survive.

Now, where was I? Somewhere in another life . . .

Barey Bhai decreed that I was to become useful in some way. They trained me for several weeks. I learned to pick pockets and extract money and valuables from handbags. Relaxed, nimble fingers. Like delicate tongs.

In and out. Like this! Always with the index and middle fingers.

Never probe.

Get whatever you can, the first time. Don't be curious. Never be greedy!

The world was once again crowded with instructions. I sulked and fretted.

Faster. Quicker! Jaldi, jaldi!

Noiseless. Inconspicuous. Glide rather than run. Retreat like a shadow. I exercised my fingers . . . walked around with weights tied to them. The consequences of failure were impressed upon me.

Slithering. Crawling. Wriggling like worms. Gradually I acquired a dexterity which made me proud and confident. My mind began to react instinctively to commands. The fingers of the right hand followed like professional fighters responding to their leader's command.

I practised with Chaman and Lightning Fingers. They coached me with meticulous care – diversionary tactics, ways of creating confusion, means of escape. Reservoirs of excuses. Words of humility and contrition. Hard-luck stories. How to bribe policemen. Cringe and fawn. I was not shrewd enough to recognize the urgency in their voices or the vague shadows of fear in their eyes.

The godown became a prison. I was not allowed to wander beyond its wasteland of rusting machinery, broken bricks, rotting timber, chains and ropes. An imperial past had left behind its silent reminders of an alien presence. Feelings of claustrophobia and loss of freedom were incentives enough to strive for proficiency beyond any natural talent for thievery. I even resorted to training at night among the monstrous shadows the candle butts projected on the walls.

Barey Bhai inquired about my progress.

Slow.

Huh? What! I thought I was already an expert.

He asked again a few days later.

Slow.

I sensed a conspiracy inspired by envy.

The same reply after another week. Barey Bhai's temper ignited, and the demon inside him raged like a monsoonal storm. He abused us for our incompetence, and then turned on himself for an unforgivable lapse of judgement.

'One more week,' he said ominously.

Chaman and Lightning Fingers doubled their efforts. They scolded, cajoled and slaved over me. 'Ay yoh, Vamana! Pay attention and try harder! We do not wish to lose you. Harder, baba . . .'

Otherwise . . . otherwise. My mind was unable to grasp the sinister implications of what was left unsaid. I was not yet wise to Barey Bhai's response to failure, or the indifference with which a life could be extinguished.

Chaman and Lightning Fingers were not much older than I. Yet their multitudinous experiences with the hazards of survival had wisened them far beyond their years. They were incapable of laughter. Beyond humour. For every action there was a motive. Behind every motive was the instinct for self-preservation. Adversity made them even more determined to cling to life, as though it was their only possession. But humanity had not deserted them. A trickle of kindness flowed from them like an underground stream in a parched land. I could not understand why they did not abandon me. For some inconceivable reason they were desperate for me to succeed. They schemed and concocted, sweated and lied.

Before the fateful week ended, I was declared efficient enough to be unleashed in the narrow lanes and crowded bazaars of Old Delhi. Another few days without the exaggerations of my progress and, I was to discover much later, my mangled, decomposed body might have been accidentally found in a canal or an open field. No identification. No one to claim the corpse. A brief stop by a police van. Hastily scribbled notes. No formal inquiry. A sparse report destined for a quiet disappearance among the thousands of unsolved cases. The eradication of a worthless life, among the hundreds of millions, could hardly be expected to create a fuss.

Chandni Chowk. Hot. Dusty. Smelling of offal, urine, stale cooking-oil and poverty. Once the pride of Moghul opulence. It should have been allowed to die with dignity, its life stored in stories and the memories of successive generations.

Half past nine. The Moonlight Bazaar was already overflowing with shoppers and bargain hunters, vendors and curious tourists.

'Vamana, jaldi karo!'

I had stopped near a stall crammed with plastic trinkets, glass bangles and costume jewellery.

'Memsaheb, you like lovely model of Taj Mahal? You want? Special price for you!'

'Dhig, dhig . . . Dhung dhig! Watch the monkey's dance! So so wonderful this morning's tamasha!'

'You want carpet? Silk, wool, Persian, Kashmiri! Moghul antique? Old daggers? Rajputana swords?'

'Sexy films? Women and men? Men with boys? Women and girls? No problems! Whatever satisfies!'

'Hot pakoras and sweets! Sherbet made from ancient and secret recipes! Guaranteed to keep you cool from the day's heat. Ek dum! Pucca promise! Money back!'

A one-eyed man harassed two embarrassed male goras. 'You fuckey fuckey? Young girls! Firm breasts and tight bums. Hah? How much you pay?'

Here was the living story of India. Beggars, snake-charmers, ear-cleaners, barbers, fortune-tellers, tea shops, stalls crammed with dazzling coloured garments. Cows munching on the mounds of rotting vegetables. Squatting children shitting behind the stalls. Crows, dogs, pedlars. Nothing orderly, nothing safe.

Excitement subdued the initial nervousness about the impending trial of my efficiency. Time peeled off its mask to reveal the grandeur of an imperial past.

A buzzing noise. The past began to speak in seductive voices. How could the mind remain dormant? I chased the years away . . .

Dust and rubble. Bare-bodied workers toiled under a relentless sun. A large pool at the centre of the square. The water rippled under a full moon. Chandni Chowk, as it was. Ali Mardan Khan's canal flowed with sweet, unpolluted water to feed the pool built by Begum Saheb. Jahanara, the Emperor's favourite daughter. Part of the seventh city of Delhi.

There! The grandeur of imperial processions. Bejewelled elephants and Arabian stallions. Splendidly dressed noblemen with their slaves in attendance. I was among them in silken robes and a muslin turban studded with rubies and emeralds, astride a white horse. The weight of pearls and gold marked me as a prince, a dwarf prince . . . Well, one of the emperor's illegitimate sons, perhaps?

An endless pageant! Music. Dancing. Magical shows. Fire-eaters and fakirs who pierced themselves with swords and walked on beds of burning coal. Pigeon racing and poetry competitions. Celebrations of a regal life dedicated to worldly pleasures and wastage. The gaiety and . . . yes, the inevitable sadness. The cruelties and destructive energies of conquerors. Communal groans of suffering. Curses. Spells. Lies and intrigues. Hoards of ghosts and vengeful spirits plotting downfalls by stirring worldly ambitions.

Hoofs pounded across the parched land and raised the dust of ephemeral achievements. The history of Delhi was the history of the world. Its timeless eyes witnessed the procession of centuries. And I saw it all . . .

Dynasties and emperors. The massacre of Delhiwallahs by the Qizalbash thugs of Nadir Shah. Ahmed Shah Abdali's invasion and the tyranny of Ghulam Qadir Ruhela. The fearless raids of Jats and Mahrattas. Such loss! The Peacock throne being carried away. Gora foreigners from a distant island. Glories vaporized into dreams of the past . . .

The palm of Chaman's hand stung my cheek. This was not the place for day-dreams. Shrewd eyes had spotted a victim.

'Vamana!' Lightning Fingers whispered, nodding in the direction of an old lady haggling over the price of watermelons. She carried a tatty handbag.

I continued to walk ahead, ignoring the glares which threatened painful retributions. Twists and turns. I enjoyed leading them into confusion. Leadership roles had suddenly changed.

'Vamana! Barey Bhai won't be pleased! Vamana?'

I saw him in front of a stall that sold sandalwood paste, soap, rouge, kajal, body oils and attar. Dressed in a saffron coloured kurta and white dhoti, he was a slender figure of irresistible sensuality. A face to set my dreams aflame. Thick lips reddened with paan juice. Long eyelashes. Glowing cheeks and delicate hands. Those long, slim fingers could have stroked away all my pain . . . Aaaaah!

A corner of a handkerchief peeked out of his kurta's pocket. My fingers would have preferred to touch his legs and caress those mounds of flesh. My legs trembled and my hands itched. Desire hardened.

Reluctantly I went around the shop and crept up behind him. A hessian bag, resting on the ground behind his right leg, caught my attention. Its bulge made me curious.

He was bargaining over the price of perfume which, the shopkeeper insisted, had been imported from Iran.

Someone brushed past me. Guiltily I turned. Scowling faces, disinterested in the dramas around them. Vendors shouted. Housewives argued. Shoppers jostled each other and kept moving. My presence did not arouse even a fleeting curiosity. I was not an oddity here among the mutilated beggars and the lepers with their bowls and cries for alms.

It was easy. Oh, so easy!

I picked up the bag and walked away. An animal panted inside me. Louder. Closer. I imagined a cry. *Thief! Chor! Stop him!* Cold hands on my neck. A crowd administering instant justice.

Nothing. I squeezed through a narrow opening between two stalls and entered a less crowded by-lane. The shock of the sudden triumph was a giddy sensation. My chest puffed and I whistled an improvised tune. The noise of the bazaar receded into a distant din as I contemplated the accolades for my success. Barey Bhai's commendations. Baji's praise and prayers of thanksgiving. The astonishment of Hira and Nimble Feet. Lightning Finger's dance of delight. Chaman and Farishta . . . quietly contented. I had proved myself. I was among the best.

Back in the godown I waited patiently, disciplining myself not to open the bag. It was several hours before I heard their voices.

The silence of anger. Faces froze in disbelief as I held up the bag in a boastful display of my achievement.

Chaman reached me first. She grabbed my shoulders and shook me violently. Abuses. Accusations. Incoherent yelling. Voices bounced off the walls and assaulted me. Dark memories. Vijay stared at me. Strange noises bubbled from within. I broke loose and receded to the tangle of rusty chains, iron rods and wooden planks.

'Are you mad?' Farishta shouted. 'Do you think people carry money in such large bags?'

'You must immediately hide what you take!'

'You are a danger to our safety!' Hira spoke vehemently. 'Do you realize what could have happened?'

Yes. Yes. Yes! I wasn't thinking. There was adequate space for me to crawl inside an empty tea chest lying on its side.

'Our survival depends on trust and caution!' Lightning Finger snorted. 'You do not have a life of your own here. We are a community of thieves. One identity!'

'Vamana, come out. You won't be hurt.'

I wanted to believe Chaman. I stuck my head out of the tea

chest and mumbled that I had been rash. The contrition in my voice silenced them. I emerged hesitantly.

They huddled together near the buckled doors of the godown, speaking in hushed voices. Chaman glanced at me several times and shook her head vigorously.

Suddenly beams of sunlight strayed through the perforations in the ceiling and flamed a section of the wall. My thoughts wandered to the man I had robbed. Desire ignited. A shower of sparks. I grew and soared beyond the hopelessness of my surroundings.

He lay naked on his stomach, his body exhaling a musky smell. Attar and sweat. I rubbed his back with oil. He breathed gently. Did he have hair on his chest? The idea repulsed me. I imagined a clean skin dotted with brown nipples.

You have strong hands.

Your back. It is . . . It is . . .

Beautiful? He undulated like a restless reptile. The buttocks were shaped by a divine craftsman.

Yes!

I know. You may go now.

What?

You can go.

I thought . . .

'You will say nothing to Barey Bhai. Do you understand?' Chaman stood protectively over me and peered into my face. 'Nothing!'

I nodded, eager to please.

'Another chance, Vamana. Last one,' Farishta warned.

Chaman spread a piece of cloth on the floor. They tossed in an assortment of items – a cigarette lighter, fountain pen, coins. An empty wallet and a packet of cigarettes. As an afterthought Chaman threw in a five-rupee note.

'Not a word!' Chaman gathered up the corners of the cloth and tied them together in a knot. 'Stay here.'

They bolted the door from the outside. I was punished with hunger and loneliness.

In their anxiety to protect me, the bag was forgotten. I dumped the contents on the floor. Two wigs. Small, brass containers of different shapes. A mirror. Several lipsticks. Wads of cotton wool. Brushes. A file. Combs. Hair clips. A booklet on make-up. Feverishly I threw them all back into the bag and carried it to the darkest part of the godown.

My sleeping corner gave me a privacy no one else wanted. Stacks of unused terracotta tiles and broken bricks created the illusion of a room. A small opening, where the tin had rusted, admitted adequate light during the day. I even had the luxury of an old mattress with several pieces of springed wire sticking out at various angles. The area was perpetually damp and smelly. I had placed the mattress tightly in the corner where the rain water didn't drip on it. But what I treasured most was a deep hole under some wooden planks which lay horizontally near the tiles.

A fortuitous discovery. I was carving my name on the floor with a nail. It slipped out of my hand and rolled under a piece of wood. The noise of a fall made me curious. I wriggled a finger through a tiny opening. Nothing. It was like hanging in space from the edge of the world. I managed to drag the planks to one side. The darkness was a night sky without the stars. Perhaps this was how God contemplated the universe before he turned on the lights. The hole gaped at me, inviting an exploration. I resisted the impulse to jump in. Mice. Cockroaches. Snakes. The imagination wandered into the possible dangers. I could not even guess how deep it was. I threw in a brick. A squelching sound. Scurrying feet. I tossed in more bricks and tiles. Silence. Soon I was able to dangle a foot over the edge and feel an uneven surface with the tip of a big toe. The hole was wide enough to swallow me. Gingerly I lowered myself into the cavity. It was fun to sit there and pretend that I was the emperor of an underworld.

I, Vamana, banish all men over two feet tall.

I, Vamana, will graciously receive all gifts, honours and adulations of my loyal subjects.

I, Vamana, promise to love the women of my domain and take a new wife every month.

I, Vamana, shall rule over this land until the sun withers and night conquers the world.

Wheee!

The hole became my treasury, my hiding ground of personal possessions I did not wish to share with others. It was to become the custodian of my secrets.

I read the instruction booklet twice and then balanced the mirror on a pile of bricks. Ooooh! The wet cotton wool felt cool on my cheeks. I patted my face with a piece of cloth and rubbed in the cream with the tips of my fingers. Powder and rouge.

Kajal. Lipstick. I worked assiduously with eager hands. The larger of the two wigs was uncomfortably tight.

The mirror. I shied away from looking into it until . . . until the urge was overwhelming.

The speechless shock of a first meeting. The eyes lowered. The pulse quickened.

The face – coy or genuinely shy? It looked at me kindly. I scanned it with anxiety. No traces of revulsion or laughter. I stepped closer.

My . . . my name is Vamana.

She was . . . well, not exactly beautiful . . . but fresh and sparkling.

I am Kamini. I am from the timeless garden.

May . . . may I?

Of course. I am one of yours. Whatever pleases you.

Eyes closed, I leaned over to touch her lips. Smooth. Cold as a winter's ocean.

Will you go away with me?

Where?

Over the empty palaces and graves, across the astonished moon and beyond the jealous sun.

Only if you talk to me about things unseen.

What shall I say?

Tell me about the floating country where nothing grows old. Where the debris of ruined lives cannot crumble any further. Where the wind cries because it can only strum the vacant space. The trees are without leaves – gaunt and black. A land where restless shadows wait for memory's return.

There is no love in such a place.

Nothing to hate either.

And if I do . . . will you stay with me forever?

I cannot do the impossible.

For a lifetime then?

Only if a man doesn't come along.

But I am a man!

You are a mirage. A distorted image formed by the reflection of sour dreams in the fading afternoon's light. You are . . .

I didn't feel the pain straight away. A red streak on the cracked mirror. Then the throbbing in my right hand. I looked again.

Kamini?

She had disappeared.

Pauline Melville

A QUARRELSOME MAN

On that particular Tuesday afternoon in July, it rained. Then it stopped. Then it rained again, making the streets wet, steamy and hot. The herbalist shop in one of the shabbier districts of south London was packed with customers. One stout, black, elderly woman in spectacles and a blue felt hat was leaning across the counter whispering in the assistant's ear.

'I want sometin' for me husband. 'E caan stop goin'. 'E runnin' to the toilet all the while.' The pale assistant with the pale-rimmed glasses looked as though vegetable juice ran in her veins. She answered benignly:

'We have Cranesbill for urinary incontinence.'

'What?' The old woman screwed up her face.

'Cranesbill for urinary incontinence,' the assistant said a little louder.

'What's that? I don' hear so good.'

'Cranesbill for a weak bladder,' shouted the assistant, causing a titter in the crowd.

'Yes. Gimme some o' dat. An' some tincture of cloves for me tooth.'

The assistant made up the order briskly and neatly. Behind her on the wall hung one of the original, old-fashioned advertisements for 'Balsam of Lungwort containing Horehound and

This story concerns the chance meeting of two people of Caribbean origin who have ended up in England as a result of the diaspora. It was chosen as a tribute to those men who, for whatever reason, are bringing up children on their own.

Aniseed – A Boon to the Afflicted'. The shop had been there since the beginning of the century. In the fifties it nearly closed through lack of trade. Then the black people started to arrive. Business picked up. As word spread, African and Caribbean people from all over London came seeking poke root for sore throats; senna pods for their bowels; fever grass for their colds; green camphor ointment; slippery elm; Irish moss; Jamaican sorrel; eucalyptus leaves; until Mr Goodwin, the latest in a long line of Goodwins, far from shutting up shop, was obliged to take on two more assistants and one extra person to serve at the Sarsparilla counter.

Now, Mr Goodwin stood patiently dispensing the order of two French hippies, the only white customers, who were taking an inordinately long time browsing through the list of potions and powders and gums and roots and barks, sniffing at herbs and examining tinctures of asafoetida and red capsicum with little crooning noises of surprise and delight. They were unaware of the jostling throng of some twenty people behind them. Wedged amongst these was a small, black boy of about ten, gazing about him in astonishment. He had thickly protruding lips and his head was closely shaven. In each ear sat a grey, plastic hearing-aid the shape of Africa. The man at his side was restless and edgy. Jittery. His forehead kept wrinkling into a frown. His frizzy hair had something unkempt about it. His teeth were small and jagged. He wore a sweater, grey with a green diamond pattern on it, frayed at the neck and his trousers were old, brown and shapeless. Round his neck hung two silver chains, one carrying a small, gold box and the other a miniature pistol, which is why he was known as Pistol-Man. He looked vexed and was making small noises of dissatisfaction. When a young black woman pushed in front of him he could contain himself no longer:

'Hey! You pushin' in front of me. I don' come all the way from north London to wait at the back of the line. She pushin' in front of me,' he complained. Then he rounded indignantly on two other people he had seen edging their way towards the front.

'An' I see you pushin' in front of them.' He started to wave his arms like the conductor of a large orchestra. 'An' them people,' he indicated a mother and child at the back, 'was here before you,' he tapped on the shoulder of a pompous-looking Trinidadian with a moustache. The man shrugged him off:

'Cool it, nuh. Cool it nuh, man. Everythin' cool till yuh open yuh big mouth. There ain' no lines.'

The man with the pistol round his neck looked fit to explode:

'That's what I say. There ain' no lines.' He threw up his hands in distress as if the disorder in the shop was somehow represent-ative of all the disorder in the world; the chaos in Beirut; the turmoil in Sri-Lanka; the upheavals in the Philippines and to some extent the confusion in himself, and if only he could organise it properly, that and everything else in the world would be set to rights. Then, out of the corner of his eye, he spotted a gap in the crowd ahead of him and stepped quickly into it.

'Now you pushin' in front of me.' The tall, light-skinned woman with the red head-wrap smiled as she accused Pistol-Man. He looked abashed, mortified.

'I know,' he said, looking round the room defensively, 'but I was goin' to let you go before me. I'm fair.' He spoke loud enough for everyone to hear.

Finally, triumphantly, he reached the counter. Then he remembered the cinnamon-skinned woman in the red head-wrap:

'Do you still want to come in front of me?' he asked, politely. Vera Mullins did indeed want to be served first. She had been on duty at the hospital since six in the morning and her feet were aching.

'Yes,' she said, moving forward to address the woman behind the counter. 'It's for my friend,' she explained. 'Her glands are all swollen in her neck and under her arms.'

'We can't really treat that,' said the assistant. 'That is likely to be a symptom of something else and we would need to know . . .'

'Lavender oil,' interrupted Pistol-Man loudly from behind Vera's shoulder. 'Give she lavender oil.'

Vera Mullins began to laugh. But she bought some lavender oil anyway. As she waited for it to be wrapped, the clean smell of peppermint floated into her nostrils from somewhere, remind-ing her of her grandmother in St Vincent whose clothes always smelt of peppermint and bay rum. People in the shop were now laughing and talking noisily. That too reminded her of home and the market in Kingstown. Taking herself completely by surprise she found herself turning round to address the shoppers:

'All right,' she said. 'I driving back to Finsbury Park. Is who needs a lift in that direction – north London?' Pistol-Man was busy at the counter ordering the bitter aloes that settled his stomach after too many cans of McEwans Export Strong Lager. He cocked his ear, unable to believe his luck:

'I do,' he said quickly.

'What about those other people from Stoke Newington?' Vera pointed towards Mr and Mrs Ebanks, who were standing, rooted to the same spot, having made no progress.

'The lady says do you want a lift home?' called Pistol-Man, in his cracked voice, gesticulating over the heads of waiting customers.

'No tanks,' replied Mrs Ebanks. 'We fine. We jus' wait and take our time till it get less busy.'

'Anyone else?' asked Vera, turning her head from side to side, expectantly. Brown, almond-shaped eyes looked enquiringly from a passive, oval face. Pistol-Man was staring at Vera with a mixture of pleasure and suspicious curiosity. He fingered the day's growth of stubble on his chin and wished he had shaved that morning. Alarmed to find that Pistol-Man was the only volunteer, Vera, for an instant, regretted her offer. She could feel something fractious and nervy about the man. London was full of dangerous strangers, unlike St Vincent. No one else took up the offer. She managed a smile:

'My car's round the corner,' she said.

Outside, rain speckled the pavement like a bird's egg. They walked past the drab shops, Pistol-Man talking fast and furious as a fire-cracker to disguise his self-consciousness. Somehow, the more he prattled, the more calm Vera Mullins became.

As they rounded the corner, Vera realised that the little black boy with the deaf-aids was scurrying along behind them. Pistol-Man turned to see where she was looking:

'Oh yeah,' said Pistol-Man. 'That's my son. He's deaf and dumb from he was born. I raise him.'

It was Vera's turn to feel curious. As she unlocked the door of the old, blue Ford with rusted streaks along its side, she caught the boy looking at her. His eyes were eager, full of merriment and intelligence, as if he were about to say something of great importance. If you could speak, she found herself thinking, you would say something beautiful. Suddenly, she felt safer about giving a lift to this talkative stranger who crackled with tension.

Safer now that she knew the child would be with them.

'What's his name?' she asked.

'Avalon,' replied Pistol-Man. 'I named him that. I found it in a book of myths. I think it's Greek,' he added.

Avalon. Avalon. Where wounded heroes go to rest. Where King Arthur went to heal his wounds. The boy scrambled into the back of the car.

'Sorry. This car is a tip,' Vera apologised. Pistol-Man raised his head to the heavens and cackled incredulously. The woman saved him the fares, saved him a long tedious wait in bus queues. As if he would care about a little mess. He would have been grateful for a ride in a donkey cart. They set off through the wet street, full of litter from the market. Pistol-Man crowed with delight inside himself for having secured a ride, as if he had outwitted the Fates for once. But he talked non-stop, through a sort of shyness. He couldn't make the woman out. Because she said so little, he talked all the more. Because he did not often have the chance to talk, everything about his life and his son came out in a torrent:

'He's got five per cent hearing. He's all right. He can lip-read. He can do sign language. And he can lie as good as any normal boy,' added the father proudly. 'He's so convincing, you wouldn't believe it.' Vera glanced over her shoulder at the child who could weave falsehoods with his hands. Avalon was sitting with his head twisted round trying to look at an old magazine on the floor of the car.

'Sometimes he's sad,' continued Pistol-Man, 'because no friends come to see us. I tell him friends will come some day. I quarrelled with my family, you see. I don't see them no more. It's just me and him now. It's a good thing to have a close family.' He said it with regret, as if a family was something that had somehow passed him by, out of reach. The truth was that Pistol-Man quarrelled with everybody. He was a quarrelsome man, pig-headed, easily annoyed, impatient, fretful.

'He's at a Special School now. He's going to boarding school in September. Then I can get back to my music. I'm a musician you see. I want to form my own band. I've worked with other bands and it's no good. The people they make excuses. They don't turn up. There's too much hassle. Too much pressure. An' then I get vex, you see and I blow my top because the people them drive me mad. I can see it's goin' to happen but I can't stop it. I wish I could be six people at once, then I could be all the members of the band.'

'Dad-dee.' The hard-to-form words came from the back of

the car. Pistol-Man turned to the boy. In the driving-mirror, Vera could see the boy's hands moving like butterflies. His father signed a reply.

'You can talk sign language?' asked Vera.

'I'm not very good at it, though,' said Pistol-Man modestly. 'I just told him "Lady give lift home."'

As they edged through the rush-hour traffic, rain spotting the windscreen, Pistol-Man threw a sly, sidelong look at the woman sitting impassively at the wheel beside him.

'You could be giving a lift to a mad person,' he said. 'A killer person.'

'I trusted you because of the child.' As she spoke, Vera remembered she had offered the lift before knowing the child was with him. Pistol-Man had his face pressed to the window. She turned and smiled at Avalon who grinned with pleasure in return.

'He's all right.' Pistol-Man looked over his shoulder at the boy. 'He knows that whatever I have, he has too. We share everything. We're equal.' His head jerked round as something in the street caught his attention. 'D'you see that shop? They sell fluffy things in there that you can sit on and they roll out into sleeping bags. They're fluffy.' He said it with relish. 'I can't afford one. They're about eighty pounds.' The quietness of the woman seeped into him, soothing him. Out of the blue, he said:

'Some people calm people down. They could get attacked but it goes the other way.' He wished he had not been so loud-mouthed in the herbalist's. 'You mek fuss and people look at you as if you were mad, but if you don't mek fuss people walk all over you,' he muttered, half to himself.

'Here we are. Pull up by that tree.' The man and the boy got out of the car:

'Bye . . . Bye.' Avalon made the sounds a diver makes speaking under water.

'Just a minute. Just a minute. Would you like to come in for a drink?' Pistol-Man's forehead wrinkled into worried lines as he peered through the car window at her. She felt drawn to the man and the child. It can't do any harm, she thought.

To Pistol-Man's exasperation, the key stuck in the lock of the basement door. Avalon pulled a face at Vera that said clearly 'Oh no, not again!' Finally the key turned and they stepped into a small, dark passage and then into the back room.

'Sit down. Sit down.' He waved his guest towards an old

settee with a crumpled, stone-coloured duvet on it that he pulled over himself at nights as he lay watching television.

'Wait there a minute,' he said. 'I've got to get him his tea.' He felt awkward, unused to visitors. He disappeared into the kitchen, shutting the door behind him so that she would not see the washing-up piled in the sink. Vera looked round the room. The walls were painted yellow ochre. The furniture was cheap and ugly. On the floor was a grey carpet as thin as cardboard. On the mantel-piece rested a semi-circular mirror flanked on either side by two big, plastic Coca Cola bottles. Pistol-Man had cut the tops of these to use them as jars which held an assortment of rulers and pencils. Opposite her, under the low dresser, was a jumble of plimsolls and trainers belonging to the man and the boy. Piles of papers and folders were stashed untidily about the place. From the kitchen came the sound of something frizzling in the pan.

Pistol-Man elbowed his way into the room carrying a plate with two hamburgers on it and some spaghetti from a tin. He put the food on the formica-topped table and turned to Avalon. He spoke and used sign language at the same time:

'Go and put your pyjamas on.' He explained to Vera, 'I have to tell him to do that because he gets his clothes dirty and it's me has to wash them. Do you want a drink? I've got McEwans Lager because that's what I drink.'

'I don't drink alcohol. Have you got any juice?' She hoped this would not prove awkward for him but for a minute Pistol-Man looked flummoxed:

'Ribena,' he said, 'I've got some Ribena.' He returned from the kitchen with a tumbler so brimful of the red liquid that he nearly spilled it.

'I hope that's not too sweet. Is it too sweet?' he enquired anxiously.

'It's fine,' she said. Avalon bounced back into the room wearing a pair of white cotton pyjamas with navy-blue triangles on them. His presence relieved the sexual tension between the man and the woman. Pistol-Man straddled a chair by the table as Avalon sat down to eat his meal. He pulled the metal ring off his can of lager:

'Yeah. This is where I always am, every evening, with my cans of beer. I have to stay in, you see, because of him. He can't ever say to me "You have more fun than me because you're grown-up", because he sees that I stay in too. We both stay in. He knows that everything I have, I share with him. We're both the same. Both equal. Sometimes, he pretends to be worse than he is.' Pistol-Man put his hand to his ear and pulled a sad face, mimicking the boy. ' "I'm deaf," he says, "I'm deaf." And I say, "Yes, I know you're bloody deaf." And we both laugh.' He took a gulp of lager. 'It's a sacrifice I make, you see. No. Not a sacrifice.' He hunted for the right word. 'No. It's a dedication.' He looked over at the boy. 'I growed him and I raised him. It's like putting money in the bank. An investment. You watch it grow. Only it's love. I'm not really a materialist. I'm more a spiritual sort of man.'

More or less the only trips Pistol-Man ever made were to the betting-shop round the corner which he visited as often as possible, optimism springing afresh in his breast on every occasion. He pulled his chair round to face the woman squarely.

'Now, I'm going to interrogate you,' he said. 'What do you do?'

'I'm a nurse,' said Vera.

'Where do you come from?'

'St Vincent – a long time ago.'

'I'm from Buxton in Guyana,' he said. 'I don't remember that much either.' He scrutinised his new friend. She sipped her Ribena. Usually, he would have said to a woman like that 'You're looking nice and slim' or 'That's a nice outfit you're wearing,' but something about this woman prevented him from doing so. He took in her honey-coloured skin and slanting, serious, brown eyes. His own skin was dark.

'There's some Portuguese in my family somewhere,' he said. 'Portuguese are white people, you know.' He rolled up the sleeve of his sweater and inspected his forearm as if expecting to see white patches appear magically on the brown.

'I like you,' he said, looking directly at her. 'Yes. I like you.'

Vera thought that she should leave soon. Avalon was busy on the floor, drawing something with a ruler and pencil. Suddenly, Pistol-Man spotted the dirty plate on the table and leapt to his feet. Vera almost laughed at the tableau they made: the man pointing sternly at the plate and the boy with his eyes widening in dismay, his hand over his mouth. The boy's deafness had made both of them expressive in face and gesture, like actors in a silent movie.

'Fair's fair,' said Pistol-Man as Avalon went into the kitchen with the plate, giving Vera a broad grin as he went. 'I cook for him, but he must wash up. That's only fair, isn't it? We both share the work.'

'What happened to his mum?' Vera couldn't help asking. Pistol-Man gave an exasperated sort of sigh and shook his head:

'She left,' he said, sitting back down in his chair. 'She was a virgin when I met her, so I don't know why I went with her because I don't like virgins,' he said candidly. 'We lived in a little room in Stoke Newington. I was working as a cutter – you know – cloth – cutting cloth. Avalon was seventeen months old. She left on a Friday. Well, you know how horrible Fridays are.' He opened his arms wide as if to emphasise the horribleness of Fridays. 'You've been working all week and you're tired and you're looking forward to the weekend. Anyway, I came home and found a note stuck on the paraffin heater saying she'd gone. The baby was all pissed up in his cot. And that was that.' He frowned as though it was still a puzzle to him. 'Maybe I was a bit of a tyrant,' he said regretfully. 'But I didn't beat her or anything,' he added hastily. 'It was just that when I wanted something done, I wanted it done properly. I wanted it done the right way.' Vera could see how the man could be bossy, cantankerous even. He continued with an expression of bewildered anguish on his face:

'It's because I want people to make progress. I want things to be better. Even with him,' he gestured towards Avalon who had gone into the bathroom, 'I want him to be somebody.' He spoke with a burst of energy, enthusiasm and hope. 'I want him to be something. He can't hear and he can't speak much but I want him to be the best he can. To be his own person.' He got up and pointed out of the window. 'That's why I've let the grass grow like that.' Vera looked to where he was pointing. Outside, the grass had run wild, nearly waist-high, in the small garden. 'The neighbours keep telling me I must cut it, but it's more interesting for him like that. There's lots of things he can discover in that grass: butterflies and worms, snails and caterpillars and insects with long legs, lots of things. He can hide in it and imagine things. It's more of an adventure for him like that.'

Avalon came in and took his father by both forearms, then he bared his teeth at him.

'Yes. That's all right,' said Pistol-Man. He turned to Vera, a little shame-faced, to explain. 'I make him do that because he didn't used to brush his teeth properly. I should stop him doing that really,' he said. 'He's too old for that now. Would you like to see his drawing? He's talented. Maybe he'll get trained one day.'

He ushered Vera into the boy's bedroom. It was small and pokey. Two big wardrobes dwarfed the single bed. Over the head of the bed was a picture of Superman. On the other wall was Avalon's drawing of Elvis Presley. Vera smiled and nodded at Avalon in appreciation. Immediately, the boy jumped on the bed and tried to pull down a big folder from the top of the wardrobe, indicating that he wanted to give her all the drawings he had ever done.

'She don't want all those, silly,' said Pistol-Man. He opened the wardrobe. Inside were half a drum-kit and a battered electric guitar. 'Those are my instruments,' he said proudly. 'I'll show you my room.'

The three of them peeked into his room. Vera was made shy by the sight of his double bed, neatly made up with a plain coverlet. She glanced quickly round. On a shelf was another photograph of Avalon with two schoolfriends. There was not much else in the room. She backed out. They returned to the living-room.

'I've got to go now,' she said.

'You're shooting off then,' said Pistol-Man. In his eagerness to do what she wanted he almost ran her out of the front door.

'Call in any time you want,' he said. 'We're always in from about six o'clock. Thanks again for the lift.'

'Bye . . . Bye,' said Avalon.

Vera waved goodbye. It had stopped raining. As she drove through the cramped streets an immense and irreparable sense of loss overwhelmed her for the island where she had once lived with its whispering seas and the sound of women's voices in the soft night air, dripping slowly and unevenly like molasses; for the people she had once known.

Back in his flat, Pistol-Man slapped himself on the forehead:

'Oh no! I forgot to ask her her name.' Avalon pulled a face of commiseration. 'Not that it matters.' Pistol-Man no longer thought about women because of his dedication to the boy.

'Did you like her?' asked Pistol-Man. Avalon, his eyes shining, put his hands on his lips and then on his heart. He went back to his drawing on the floor. Pistol-Man sat on the settee and opened another can of lager. He felt good. He felt warm inside. Tomorrow, he decided, he would hoover the carpet and give the whole place a good clean-up. What luck, he thought, to get a lift home on a wet afternoon like that.

Suddenly, he leant forward and grasped his son by the arm to attract his attention. He spoke in sign language only:

'You see!' he said to the child who looked intently at him. 'Good things do happen.'

Alex Miller

THE PORTRAIT SELF

When I was old and could no longer hope for new friendships, one of the saddest episodes of my life began to come back to me and to offer me my greatest joy. Under the influence of this memory, revisiting me in its new disguise, I was able to paint again. For the gift had left me. I don't believe I'll ever suffer such a paralysis of my will again. Now I'll go on painting until the end. Which must be the hope of every artist. Simply to work.

And that is what she gave me, Jessica Keal, the subject of this altered memory, a memory entangled with certain family likenesses and forgotten moments of my childhood; her roots and mine mysteriously grown together. That entire episode is contained for me in a single image. And although there's only one figure in this image – for it's my portrait of Jessica Keal that I'm talking about – it's an image in which I'm content, for once, to recognise myself. As I remember her, I remember myself and am able to approach the last enigma of my life – my family and my childhood. That cold legacy of silence and absence.

There are things that it's impossible to express with words. Language employed to express emotion is a perversion. The records of commerce is the only honest use of written language. The rest is a cover-up. It's not words that shape our intuitions. It's not in what we say but in what we leave unsaid that we reveal the shape of our deepest motives. In the places between

This is an extract from *The Sitters* (1995), Alex Miller's fourth novel, which was short-listed for the New South Wales Premier's Award and the Miles Franklin Award.

the words. In the tacit and the implicit. In the silence beyond words. That's where we hide our truth. Behind the endless buzzing of language. The sovereignty of silence is its ambiguity.

So it always begins with a question. An uncertainty. This affair of having a portrait painted. Jessica became at once flattered, insecure, vain, unsettled, resisting. She was all at a loss and went off warmed and glowing and scheming how she was going to influence the image of her that I was to bring into being. Not herself.

How it came about was this. Being at the university one day a week I met certain people I wouldn't otherwise have met and in this way was offered commissions I wouldn't otherwise have been offered. Within a week of running into Jessica in the corridor on my way to the lift, I was offered a commission for a series of etchings to be published in a scholarly journal associated with the university. The job was the likenesses of ten eminent Australian women to accompany articles on their work and their careers. I got the offer over the phone and I turned it down flat. It didn't appeal to me. I didn't need the money. Once I would have grabbed it. But not any more. I wanted to recover. I was exhausted. But the editor of the journal forwarded the details to me through the post anyway.

Her name was on the list: Professor Jessica Keal, Visiting Fellow in the Department of History. I sat there on my high stool next to the solander in the studio staring at her name for several minutes, watching the two of us meeting in the empty corridor, watching a more responsive meeting than the real one had been. Then I made myself a cup of coffee and thought about it some more before ringing the editor of the journal and telling her I'd changed my mind and would accept the commission after all. But I hadn't really changed my mind about the likenesses. And as soon as I'd put the phone down I wished I hadn't rung the editor and I nearly rang her again to say I'd changed my mind back again. I thought of pretending someone had impersonated me the first time. I still didn't want to do the job. I knew what they'd be like. Likenesses. An invasion of eminent women! And after all I wasn't sure. I didn't know whether I might have invented that little pool of trust between myself and Jessica just to comfort myself. That so-called offer. Maybe it hadn't really been there at all. Why *would* it have been there? No doubt she was just being polite. I didn't trust my memory of the event. We invent these things, we hope so hard for them, especially when we're tired and low in spirits and in need of reassurance that it hasn't all come to an end for us. We wake up in the middle of the night and we realise some little miracle has been offered to us during the day. And when it gets light we don't trust the miracle any more, and we decide we must have imagined it. We know this kind of hope can disable us.

So I'm sitting here on the high stool in my studio with my pad held out at an angle, resting it on my knees, my glasses on the end of my nose, and I'm doing maybe my twentieth drawing of her. As I finish a drawing I flip the page over and begin a new one. I'm working quickly. She's sitting across from me on a straight-backed kitchen chair with the vertical lines of the picture stacks behind her, and she's facing the big verandah windows and looking out into my garden. She's wearing an open-necked shirt and jeans. 'What should I wear?' she asked over the phone. It's windy and the light is moving back and forth across her face from the movement of the foliage of the almond tree. I asked her at the beginning of the session if she'd keep perfectly still just for a little while. Now she's frozen into a profile. It amuses me, this anxiety on her own behalf. She doesn't want to risk me getting it wrong. Her vanity's involved. I know she's not going to look my way and I grimace at her. After a while I ask her to come around and face me. 'Look straight at me, Jessica,' I say. 'A visiting fellow in history. What kind of history?'

She starts telling me what she does. But I'm not following what she's saying. It doesn't make any sense to me. Her voice is just a background, something to let her move a bit, with her thoughts and her search for the words. She's started thinking about history and has forgotten to look her best. This is our first meeting. I've taken the likenesses of the other nine women. She's the last. I don't muck around with things like this. I grab as much information as I can in one sitting and that's that. My idea with likenesses is always to get the thing done and to move on to something else. There's always enough from one session for me to do a passable etching or a linocut. And that's what I do. I keep it brief.

I've nearly finished. She's been here three hours. An hour longer than any of the others had. We took a break for coffee. While I was getting the coffee she had a bit of a look around the studio, respectful, keeping her distance. And that was it. There's no sense of anything going on between us. There's this decision of restraint. Just two professional people getting on with the thing they have to do. That's the way we're doing it. But there's an edginess, as if there might be something else that we're *not* dealing with. I can't be sure whether I'm imagining this. It's hard to know. No doubt it's something to do with the delicate physics of desire, which can just as easily become the physics of boredom or revulsion.

I stop drawing and say, 'Thanks Jessica. That's it,' and I close the pad and put it on the solander behind me. Businesslike. I'm a busy man. We're both busy people. We don't want to waste each other's time. She gets off the stool and stretches and comes over and asks me, 'Can I have a look?'

I pick up the pad and turn it over, face down. She waits for me to offer it to her. She's not sure of me. She's tense. Then it dawns on her.

'Aren't you going to let me see?'

She's a bit incredulous. Her colour has heightened. Her eyes are dark brown and steady and she's looking at me as if she's wondering whether I'm a reasonable man or some kind of crank.

'There's nothing to see yet,' I say.

I don't really know anything about her. I've finished getting my information for the likeness. That's all it's going to be, a likeness. I don't know the first thing about her. I know less about her now than I did when I walked into the common room where they were having the welcome for her and she looked across the room and we saw each other for the first time. In a way we knew everything about each other then. Now we know nothing. She'll be out of the studio in a minute and that'll be that. I might go on having regrets for ever. We'll nod to each other if we meet in the corridor. 'Hi', we'll say. 'How's it going?' And there'll be that awkwardness between us because nothing was ever said.

I put the pad of drawings in the solander and close the drawer.

She stands in front of me and challenges me. 'Why won't you let me have a look?'

She's disappointed. She's angry with me. She's eager to see

what I've done. She thinks she's been patient and deserves to have a look. That's *why* she's been patient, so she can claim her likeness from me at the end of the session. And there's her vanity. What have I seen, she's wondering? The likenesses are hers, that's what she thinks. She'd be confused, she might even feel misrepresented, if she saw what I've done. I've taken something from her, however, there's no getting away from that, and I've tucked it away in my solander out of her reach, in a place that's private to me. Her likeness. She's looking at me hoping I'll relent. I can feel how closed my features have become. Not that I mean to be this closed. It's just the way I am. It's being an artist that's done it. Keeping things to myself in case they lose their charge. So I close off. Especially when I'm working. I can't help it. I wish I could be light and open and friendly.

But I can't do that.

She's seen it's no use trying to be angry with someone she doesn't know and who is this closed. She sees that anger's not going to work. And I watch her beginning to slide away with this realisation, going away completely, becoming unknown, making up her mind, her small anger turning towards dislike instead of disappointment. She's beginning to believe she's been mistaken about me.

'Well,' she says, and she smiles, a stiff little smile that suggests the possibility of contempt. 'Thanks. It was interesting.'

She's leaving. I'm following her down the steps from the verandah into the garden. She's on the path and I'm still on the middle step when I say, 'I'd like to paint your portrait sometime, Jessica.'

I'm looking down at her. She turns abruptly and looks up at me, the words catching her. She's completely thrown. We look at each other. A big question is in her eyes. It might be too late. Then she looks away, her hand seeking the rail, slipping over the weathered timber, her fingertips lingering against the open grain, both of us looking at her hand, at her fingers playing over the surface of the weathered timber.

I see she knows that a portrait means something big and different and difficult. That it will not be easy. I see she knows that a portrait may fail. That it might be a project between us that fails. *Sometime* I said, so the thing's not certain. It hasn't been locked down. But she's been taken off-guard. She's flattered. She's confused now. Her vanity's been brought into it again. It's not over yet. It's unsettled her and something in her wants to resist the whole business. But she's already standing a little straighter, beginning to re-imagine herself in her own likeness, testing the thing out, preparing herself, watching a new visualisation of herself coming into being. A full portrait. She's unsteadied. She's seeing all the portraits she's ever seen and she's wondering which one will be her. And she's not sure whether she wants to accept these possibilities.

'A portrait?' she enquires, as if this is something she has never considered before. 'How long will it take?' She looks concerned as she asks this so that I won't notice that she's flattered. So that I'll think she's worried about finding the time in her busy life to sit for a portrait. She's pretending not to have understood anything, pretending she doesn't understand and may not be able to spare her attention for this kind of thing, pretending there's something here that only a painter would understand about a portrait.

'I don't do one picture,' I say. 'I do several.' It's a warning. I don't want her to get the wrong idea. 'Hundreds maybe. Some small, some not so small. And a few big ones. And drawings and etchings and woodcuts. Whatever I need. Photographs. I never know what I'm going to do. I keep several paintings on the go at once.'

She smiles at this, as if I might be teasing her, looking up at me from the bottom step, allowing herself to hope a little that maybe there's something after all. And I laugh. 'It's like that.' I say. 'It might take a year. Two years. Who knows?' A portrait has never taken me two years and I say this knowing it to be a lie. I don't mean to mislead her. But I find myself lying to her, freely, as if I'm describing something I believe in. I'm describing the future. I don't know this at the time of course, but that's what I'm doing, describing my future practice.

Suddenly, she says, surprised and offering an apology, 'I've left my bag in your studio.'

'Your cigarettes are in it,' I say.

Everyone has to satisfy their curiosity about the image. They can't help themselves. If you're writing they don't take any notice of you. If you're writing they leave you alone. But if you're drawing they have to come over and have a look over your shoulder. It's got something to do with the difference between the image and the word. The image is more primitive, it's more archaic and more direct and more public than the word. The image belongs to everyone. You can't keep it private. It jumps at us from ten thousand years ago from rock shelters in Arnhem Land and caves in Europe and from billboards on the side of the highway. When we see a drawing we all think we know what we're looking at. But the word is private. It's harder to get at. We're prepared to be puzzled. The word is more of a secret sign than the image. Antique inscriptions mean nothing to us. We need the genius of Champollion to decipher the Rosetta Stone for us, specialist knowledge, before we get any-where near the meaning of the word. And it's a delicate matter. Words are not firmly attached to their meanings. If we're clumsy and push them too hard their meaning slips out and we're left with the husk. The empty sign. If we're writing it could be our diary or a love letter or a shopping list and it's no one's business but our own, but if we're drawing it's a matter for public concern. She couldn't understand at first that these preparations belonged to me and were private. If I'd let her see them they'd have changed. They would have become something between us. I didn't try to explain. Then I surprised myself. I threw her the idea of a portrait before I'd had time to consider what I was saying. And when she'd got her bag and we were back in the studio, the wind whipping through the open door and making her hair blow around her face, she agreed.

I had a view of my garden through the large windows that enclosed the verandah. I'd let the garden grow wild. The previous owners had planted fruit trees. Apples and pears and plums. And the almond-tree. So there was this neglected orchard outside my windows where the birds came in the autumn to eat the fruit. Down the hill were the tall Lombardy poplars bordering the reserve, and then the old gum-trees they'd left standing.

No one who has a choice chooses to live in Canberra. I'm no exception. I didn't choose to live in Canberra but I had long ago decided that I'd probably never move away. My wife had been with the Department of Foreign Affairs. That's why we moved to Canberra in the first place. I was the one who'd stayed. Our son grew up there. After Jessica Keal had gone that day I stood by the window looking into the garden for a long time. I didn't

know what to think. I didn't know why I'd told her I wanted to
do her portrait.

It was a hot summer afternoon and I could hear children
screaming down at the reserve. My house was quieter than usual
and the garden emptier. I felt I might be making it all up between
us. Just inventing something out of desperation. I was tired. My
work was going through a stale patch and I wondered where I
was going to get the energy from for this portrait. Even then,
however, I detected a kind of intuitive stubbornness in myself
about it, a dumb, inarticulate resolution at a great depth, which
said there were no arguments and that I was going to go through
with her portrait no matter what. This was really the first inkling
I had that she was going to change things for me . . .

A while later Jessica brought me some family snapshots. 'That's
all there are,' she said. They were in an old tin from her mother's
place. There were one or two letters and some postcards in the
tin as well as the snapshots. The postcards were from her from
London, addressed to her mother in the Araluen Valley. I pinned
the photos on the wall above the solander and we looked at
them. A proof of the etching I'd done for the journal was lying
on the solander. While I pinned up the photos she examined the
proof, turning it round in her hands, holding it off, squinting at
it, trying it this way then that way.

'Do you like it?' I asked, observing her, wanting her to like it.
It was the first time an artist had taken her likeness. She didn't
know what to think. It disturbed her to see this image that was
her and not her. Seeing herself as strange, flat and familiar for
the first time. Disquieted by the little gulf of detachment opened
for her by the print. The printed drawing. The intimate sign of
my hand moving across the page. A touch she'd scarcely felt. A
reproduction. Once removed. Twice removed. She didn't know
how to approach it. Screwing up her face in an effort to *see* into
the likeness a feeling of herself in there. The two-dimensional
image calling her in and warding her off at the same time. The
likeness getting in the way of seeing anything at all. Nothing to
see. The likeness being unforgiving, revealing everything. Con-
cealing everything. Her eyes were like cold discs. It was another
woman. She wanted to ask me if I really saw her this way, if
people, if *everyone*, saw this woman when they saw *her*. But she
held back the question and kept it to herself. I watched her.

She turned to me. 'Perhaps you get used to it.'

'It's only a likeness,' I said, and I took it out of her hand and slipped it into the drawer.

It's the art of misrepresentation. The art of unlikeness. That's why it's so difficult. No one really knows how to do it. It's all guesswork. You've got to avoid the authority of the likeness. You can't afford to be trapped by that. You've got to slip past the likeness and close your eyes to it. You've got to reach into the dark and touch something else. The problem is always to visualise the person. Portraiture is an act of faith. In portraiture it's the shy beast you're after not the mask. Beauty and the Beast. You've got to entice the beast out of hiding into the open, past the gentle contours of the familiar. You've got to be patient and wait till it makes a move. If you rush things you'll scare it and it'll never come out. You have to gain its trust. You have to put yourself in danger. You have to offer it something of yourself. You have to take a risk.

That's not the whole truth, of course.

Portraiture's a dangerous business. It's fraught with misunderstanding. I slipped the etching into the drawer. I didn't offer to give her an impression. I didn't want her likeness coming between us. That's the mistake we make, to look for the perfect image. That's Greek philosophy. It's the antique error. The error of monotheism. It gets you nowhere. The longing for a fixed truth resident behind the reality we've brought into being ourselves. That's futility. The fallacy of the Western intellectual tradition, the idea of perfection. As if our reality is going to hold forever, in there somewhere if only we can get to it, if only we can dig deep enough, a hard impermeable kernel of truth that will hold out against the apocalypse of our loss of faith.

I closed the drawer. 'It's the signature they want from me these days,' I said. 'Likenesses are all alike.'

She wasn't sure whether I was mocking her or not. That's how careful you have to be. You have to think before you speak. It takes two to make a portrait. And one of them's always yourself.

Rohinton Mistry

THE SCREAM

The first time I heard the scream outside my window, I had just fallen asleep. It was many nights ago. The sound pierced the darkness like a needle. Behind it, it pulled an invisible thread of pain.

The night was suffocating. There was no sign of rain. The terrible cry disturbed the dry, dusty air, then died in silence. Bullies, torturers, executioners all prefer silence. Exceptions are made: for the sounds of their instruments, their own grunts of effort, their victims' agony. The rest is silence. No wisdom like silence. Silence is golden. I associated silence with virtuous people. Or at least harmless, inoffensive people. I was thinking of Trappist monks, of gurus and babas who take vows of silence. I was wrong. Even at my great age, there are many things to learn.

The scream disturbed no one inside the flat. None in the building opened a window and poked out a curious head. The buildings across the road were also hushed. The light of the street lamp grew dimmer. No witnesses?

Could I have dreamt it? But the scream was followed by shrieks: 'Bachaaav, bachaav!' yelled the man, help me, please! I opened my eyes, and there were more screams. Frightened, I shut my eyes. It was utterly horripilating. He appealed to his tormentors. I was afraid to rise and look out the window. He begged them to stop hitting, to please forgive, 'Mut maaro, maaf karo!'

That was many nights ago. But as soon as it gets dark and the light is switched off, I can think of nothing else. If I do think of something else, sooner or later the scream returns. It comes like

a disembodied hand to clutch my throat and choke my wind-
pipe. Then it becomes difficult to fall asleep, especially at my
age, with my many worries. Signs of trouble are everywhere.
The sea-gulls keep screeching. The seedlings are wilting and
ready to die. The fishermen's glistening nets emerge from the
sea, emptier than yesterday. All day long there is shouting and
fighting. Buses and lorries thunder past. Politicians make loud
speeches, fanatics shriek bloodcurdling threats. And even at
night there is no peace.

I sleep on a mattress on the floor, in the front room. In the
front room the light is better. The dust lies thick on the furniture.
The others use the back room. My place used to be there, too,
among them. All night long I could hear their orchestra of wind
instruments, their philharmonia of dyspepsia, when, with the
switching off of the lights, it was as if a conductor had raised
his baton and given the downbeat, for it started immediately,
the breathing, snoring, wheezing, sighing, coughing, belching,
and farting. Not that I was entirely silent myself. But at least my
age gives me the right; pipes grown old cannot remain soundless.
In that caliginous back room, verging on the hypogean, with its
dark nooks and corners, often the air would be inspissated
before half the night was through. And yet, it was so much
better than being alone, so much more comforting to lie amidst
warm, albeit noisy, bodies when one's own grew less and less
warm day by day.

Horripilating . . . caliginous . . . hypogean . . . inspissated . . .
It pleases me that these words are not lost on you. But you
wonder why I use them when gooseflesh, and gloomy, or hot
and steamy, would work just as well instead. Patience. I am no
show-off. Though I will readily admit that if words like these sit
inside me unused for too long, they make me costive. A periodic
purge is essential for an old man's well-being. At my age, well-
being is a relative concept. So I repeat, I am no exhibitionist,
this is not a manifestation of logorrhoea or wanton sesquipeda-
lianism. At my age, there is no future in showing off. There are
good reasons. Patience. Soon you will know.

All my life I have feared mice, starvation, and loneliness. Now
that loneliness has arrived, it's not so bad. But I knew the others
did not want me among them. For some reason I was a nuisance.
So now I sleep in the front room, on a mattress on the floor,
wedged between the sofa and the baby grand. I am in a tight
spot. One wrong turn and I could bruise a knee or crack my

forehead. The others were only too glad to see me go. They even lay out my stained and lumpy mattress for me each night. Once, I pointed to the servant and said to them, 'Let him carry it.'

'He is not a servant, he is our son,' they said, 'don't you recognize your own grandchild?'

Such liars. Always, such lies they tell me, to make me think I am losing my mind. And they carry my mattress, wearing their supererogatory airs, as if concerned about an old man's welfare. But I know the truth hiding in their hearts. They are poor actors. They think at my age I can no longer separate the genuine from the spurious, the real from the acted, so why bother to make elaborate efforts to dissimulate. But they will know, when they are old like me, that untangling the enemy's skein of deceit becomes easier with the passing of time.

With your permission, I will give you an example. Sometimes I find it difficult to rise from my chair. So I call the servant: 'Chhokra, give me a hand.' If his masters are not watching, he comes at once. If they are, he ignores me, naturally, not wanting to cross them. Taking a leaf from their book, he even mocks me. I wonder why they spoil him so much. Good servants are hard to find, yes. But to let him eat with them at table? Sleep in the same room, on a bed? And for me a mattress on the floor. What days have come. Whole world turning upside down.

My excuse for moving to the front room was to read till late in the night. In the back room they would switch off the lights; they used to say my old eyes were too weak to read past midnight, I must rest, I must not go blind, I must see my grandson grow and marry and have many children. But my eyes were quickly forgotten as they carried out my torn, stained, lumpy mattress. 'Whatever pleases you,' they said, 'we are here on earth only to serve our elders.' Huh!

In the front room, sometimes I read, but more often, after switching off the light, I go to the window. There is a deep cement ledge on the inside. I sit on the ledge. Never for more than a few minutes, though. The cement is hard on my bones, on my shrivelled old arse of wrinkled skin-bags. But once it was firm and smooth and bouncy. Once it was a bum that both men and women enjoyed gazing after. Not as deep as a well, nor as wide as a church door, thank God, but just the right size. Without blackheads or pimples, without any blemishes or irregularities whatsoever. Firm and smooth and bouncy are the precisely operative words. Not bouncy like a young woman's, but just enough, so that if you were to slap or squeeze it in a friendly manner, both of us would feel good.

The cement feels cool to the touch. You might think that a blessing in this hot climate. I don't. Not when I am craving warmth. Would you believe me if I told you the ones in the back room chill the ledge with slabs of ice, just to harass me?

But the window is convenient for making water at night. The water closet is through the back room, and if I stumble past after the others are asleep, cursing and screaming follow me all the way. There are some bushes outside the window. The neighbourhood dogs use them. They do not mind me. An old man's water is pure H_2O – no smell, no colour. Nothing much left inside me, neither impurities nor substance.

I used to keep a large old milk bottle. I'd labelled it Nocturnal Micturition Bottle, just to avoid mistakes, so no one might use it for something incompatible. The ones in the back room said I had spelt it wrong, that it should be 'micturation', a-t-i-o-n, not i-t-i-o-n. Their audacity is immedicable. When I was young (and they were little), they used to ask me for meanings, spellings, explanations. I inculcated the dictionary habit in them. Now they question my spelling.

Like you. Yes, don't deny it. I see you reaching for the OED. No need to be so sneaky, do it openly and proudly, it is one of the finest acts. To know the word, its spelling, the very bowels of its meaning, the womb which gave it birth – this is one of the few things left in life still worth doing.

Something strange happened after I began keeping the milk bottle. The volume of water I passed increased night by night. The one bottle was no longer enough. It would not surprise me if the others were slipping a diuretic into my food or medicine to torment me. Soon there were six milk bottles standing in a row at the foot of my mattress each night, all duly labelled. They were always full before the sun rose. At the crack of dawn I emptied them down the toilet bowl. I felt a pang of loss. Was there no better use for it? If the nations of the Third World were to piss in unison, the land mass of the First World just might disappear under a sea of urine. We could all take diurectics for a successful flood. Events thenceforth would be classified as ante-urinal or post-urinal. A long-overdue chapter in history could begin at last.

But one night, a bottle slipped through my fingers while micturating. Wet shards of glass glinted on the floor. The others went on for days about it. My hands keep shaking because of this disease I have. They tell me there is no cure for it. Should I believe them? The doctor said the same thing, granted. But how long does it take to bribe a doctor, slip him a few rupees?

The first night of the scream, I was not reading, or sitting on the window ledge, or micturating. I was asleep. Then the scream rose again in the street, the man begged for mercy. There was no mercy. He pleaded with them to be careful with his arm, it would break. It only goaded them to more cruelty. He screamed again. Still no one awoke. Or they pretended not to.

Why do I have to listen to this, I asked myself. If only I could fall asleep again. So difficult, at my age. Oh, so cruel, finding sleep after long searching, only to have it slip away. And afterwards? Only this – my scourge of worries and troubles. Sadhus agitating for a trade union. Cows spurning grass from strangers' hands. The snake charmer's flute enraging the cobra. Stubborn funeral pyres defying the kindling torch.

I shivered and sweated, afraid to rise from between the sofa and the baby grand to look out the window. An upright would have made more sense than a baby grand, I thought. Lying in the dark on the mattress, I could reach the pedals with my feet, and lift my arms to tickle the ivories, joining distantly in the back-room orchestra of wind instruments.

Once upon a time, I took piano lessons. I practised on this very baby grand. But after the second lesson my right-hand fingers were caught in a lift. Its doors, made from a mighty oak, closed on my hand. I did not scream. When I removed my fingers they were a good bit flattened. I smiled embarrassedly at my fellow passengers in the lift. There was no pain. My first thought was to restore the proper shape. I squeezed and kneaded the crushed fingers, comparing them to the undamaged left hand, to make sure I was achieving the correct contours. I could hear faint crunches. Then I fainted.

If I listen hard, I can still hear those crunches of my bone fragments when I flex my fingers. Flexed in time and rhythm, they resemble dim castanets. I can do the Spanish Gypsy Dance and Malaguena. Nowadays, the only person who plays the piano is the servant boy. Makes no sense to me. A piano for a servant, denying my mattress the floor space.

The other night a mouse ran over my ankles as I lay on the mattress. That was not unusual. Almost every night a mouse brushes my hands or feet. What was unusual was my feeling comforted by its touch. Happily, disgust and revulsion soon followed the pleasant sensation. Unusual responses can be disconcerting in old age. Never know what might happen next. I hated mice as a young man. I prefer to keep hating them as an old one. This way, the world stays a safer place.

Did you know that mice can nibble human toes without causing pain or waking the sleeper? The saliva of mice induces local anaesthesia and promotes coagulation, curbing excessive bleeding. Their exhaled breath, blown with expert gentleness on the digits in question, is quite soothing till the morning comes.

I tell the ones in the back room about the mice, about my fears. They don't care. No doubt they would be pleased if one morning I woke up missing a few fingers or toes. They laugh at me. Whatever I say is for them a laughing matter, worthless rubbish. I am worthless, my thoughts are worthless, my words are worthless.

One day I lost my temper. 'Floccinaucinihilipilificators!' I screamed at them. Not comprehending, they laughed again, assuming I had lapsed into the galimatias of senescence.

You seem like very sensible people for not laughing. Doubtless you have also run into a mouse or two. If my knowledge of zoology, particularly the feeding habits of *Mus musculus*, impresses and interests you, I could tell you more. It does? Say no more. We shall return to it presently.

The screams on the street gave way to groaning. There were muffled thuds, blows landing on unprotected parts. Diaphragm, kidneys, stomach. Groaning again, then violent retching. I was sweating, I trembled, I wished it would end. The air was parched. If only there were thunder and rain. If there were screaming, and also thunder and rain, it might be bearable, I thought.

The mice leave the piano alone. They never run over the keys or romp among the wires and hammers. I keep hoping to hear plinks, plonks, and musical sounds in the night not of my making. Expectations created long, long ago by children's stories, I suspect. They have turned out to be lies, like so much else.

Flying cockroaches are as terrifying as mice. But the secret is to keep a cool head when the whirring comes close to your face. Switch on the light, take a slipper, stand absolutely still instead of flailing wildly, and then, when its flight pattern becomes predictable, kill it on the wing. It's not as difficult as it sounds. I am proud to do it so well at my age. Flying or non-flying, cockroaches hold no fear for me. No, it is the insidious mouse with its anaesthetic saliva and soothing suspirations that I dread when darkness falls.

One night – another one, not the night of the scream, or the night of the soft and pleasing mouse – when I looked through the window, around midnight, unable to sleep as usual, a chanawalla came from the direction of Chaupatty, from the beach, his basket hanging from a sling round his neck. I smelled quantities of gram and peanuts in the basket. A tin can with its mixture of chopped onions, coriander, chilli powder, pepper, and salt, along with a slice of lemon, added its aroma to the dry, rainless air. My mouth was watering.

The ones in the back room have forbidden me all spices. They say the masala causes a sore throat, tonsilitis, diarrhoea; and the burden of these sicknesses will fall on their heads, they say. So they give me food insipid as saliva. And it always has too much salt or no salt at all. Deliberately, believe me. In the beginning it made me a little cross; I would yell and scream and throw the food about. Then I realized this was exactly what they wanted to see, to starve me to death. I abruptly changed my tactics. Now, the worse the food, the more I praise it. Their disappointed faces, deprived of the daily spectacle, are a sight. Of course they pretend to be glad that I am enjoying the food.

And their tricks do not stop at food. Even my medicine they deprive me of, disregarding the schedule prescribed by the doctor. Then, when my hands and feet shake more than ever, they point to them and say, 'See how sick you are? Let us take care of you. Be good, listen to what we say.' Such wickedness. Such tyranny. But I will get the better of them. One of these days they will forget to hide the key to my cupboard. Then I will be dressed and gone to my solicitor before they can say floccinaucinihilipilification.

The silhouette of the chanawalla and his neck-slung basket made me yearn for something. I could not identify the object of my yearning. He had a little wire-handled brazier to roast the peanuts. A bit of charcoal glowed in the brazier. I wished I could reach through the window and feel the warmth of that ember.

The chanawalla was accosted by three men. They jostled him viciously, though at first they seemed like friends. They grabbed handfuls of peanuts and brazenly sauntered off. When the chanawalla walked under a street lamp, I saw tears on his face. It might have been sweat. He lifted a hand and wiped his face. Once my eyes were stronger than today. Strong and piercing was my gaze. Never a chance of confusing tears and sweat.

The men who sleep outside the building across the road were still awake when all this happened. But they did not intercede on the chanawalla's behalf. Most of them are very muscular fellows. They went about preparing for sleep as if nothing was happening. They might have been right. It is hard, at my age, to know if anything is happening.

Watching the muscular fellows is my favourite pastime at this late hour. There is always laughing and joking as they unroll their bedding, strip down to their underpants, and take turns to use the tap in the alley beside the building. Pinching and slapping, pushing and shoving, they prepare for bed. Some of them share a bedding with a friend, and cuddle under a threadbare cloth, hugging and comforting. I know what it is like, the yearning for comfort. Sometimes a woman appears. She spends a little time with each of them, then departs.

Unlike the building I live in, the one across the road includes a private nursing home, an accountant's office, residential flats, a twenty-four-hour horoscope and astrology service, a furniture store, restaurant, auto shop, and a godown in the basement whose windows look out at street level. Periodically, lorries with various gods and slogans painted on their sides arrive at the building. The muscular men load or unload the lorries during the day. They work at a flat, per-lorry rate, always in high spirits.

Sometimes the prime minister visits from the capital to consult the astrologer about a favourable time for introducing new legislation, or an auspicious month for holding general elections. Then the police cordon off the area, no one can pass in or out of the building. There are long traffic jams. People who want to obtain their rations, take children to school, give birth, or go to hospital have to wait till the prime minister has finished with the nation's business.

The men who own the lorries also ask the astrologer's advice for a propitious time. The muscular men do not quibble about this. On the contrary, they are grateful: when the business was owned by unbelievers who did not take necessary precautions, a huge crate slipped and killed one of the muscular men.

On days when the stars forbid the loading of lorries, the men sit and watch the traffic. Once, on just such an idle day, a beggar stole a bun from the restaurant. The waiters gave chase to impress their manager. They caught the beggar and thrashed him soundly before he could bite the bun. A policeman ran up to deliver the obligatory law-enforcement blows. The sun was very bright and hot. I was not squeamish about watching. I am not frightened of physical pain inflicted on others. Especially if it is in moderation. And there was nothing excessive about this action. Not like the police in that very backward north-eastern state, poking rusty bicycle spokes in suspected criminals' eyes, and then pouring in sulphuric acid. Not like that at all.

The waiters took back the mangled bun. The muscular men produced a coin. They insisted that the beggar return to the restaurant and purchase the comestible with dignity. They stood around him, satisfied, and watched him eat it.

But the muscular men do not go to the rescue of the screamer. I cannot understand it. Nor can I understand, given my un-squeamish nature, why I cannot endure the screaming any more, the cries which occur at intervals every night, after midnight. I am shivering, my sweat is cold, the night is dark, my knees are aching, my brow is feverish, I am running out of things like mice, cockroaches, chanawallas to occupy my mind, the scream and pain keep displacing them. The neighbour's dog begins to bark.

Brownie begins to bark. Brownie is the brother of a dog called Lucky, who died of rabies. The others in the back room are fond of dogs, but blame me for their not being able to keep one. I would trip over the dog, they say, I would trip and fall and break my bones, and the burden of my broken bones would land squarely on their unprotected heads, they say.

Sometimes they bring Brownie in from next door to play with him and feed him the bones they save at mealtimes. Nowadays, they won't let me suck the marrowbones. They snatch them from my plate for Brownie. Even my marrow-spoon has been hidden away. The reason? A tiny bone splinter might choke me, they say. Always they have an excuse ready for the eyes and ears of the world. They try to teach Brownie to shake hands. The crotch-sniffing cur is not interested. He sticks his snout in my groin and knocks my onions around, like a performing seal. They, my onions, that is, hang lower and lower each day. Great care must be taken every time I sit. What I would not give to have again my scrotum tight as a fig. The indignities of old age.

Shrinking cucumber, and enlarging onions. What fate. But that's the way the ball bounces.

What destiny. Everything is my fault, according to the ones in the back room. They are so brave when it comes to mistreating and subjugating an old man. They want to hear no more about the scream, they threaten me, it is all my imagination. Every day they tell me I am mad, crazy, insane. That I have lost my mind, my memory, my sense of reality.

But you be the judge. You form your own opinion. Weigh the evidence. Listen to my words, regard the concinnity of my phrases. Observe the elegant coherence of my narrative. Consider the precise depiction of my pathetic state. Does this sound like a crazy man's story? Does it?

Of course not. Take a minute, later on, I beseech you, to plead my case with the ones in the back room. It is no more and no less than your duty. Apathy is a sin. This old age did not come upon me without teaching me virtue and vice. I speak the truth. I keep my promises. I am kind to the young and helpless. The young are seldom helpless.

Apathy is a sin. And yet, not one of them goes to help the screamer. How they can bear to sleep through it, night after night, I don't know. But what heroes they were, that morning, when we found a harmless drunkard under the stairs. He was asleep, clutching a khaki cloth bag containing three hubcaps. Stolen, everyone proclaimed at once. They shook him awake. Neighbours came to look. They asked him questions. He did not wish to answer. They kicked the desire into him. When he answered, they could not understand his thick-tongued mumbles. But they have seen too many movies, so of course they kicked him again. Blubbering, he took out a screwdriver from his pocket. 'I am a mechanic,' he explained. Murderer, they shouted, poking him over and over with his screwdriver. Somebody suggested he was dangerous, and should be tied up. So one of the heroes got some string. It was the flat kind, like a thin ribbon, with print on it: Asoomal Sweets, Made Fresh Daily, it read. They tied him with it, trussed him like a stuffed bird.

Oh, what heroes. Not one dares to go out and look. The screams keep coming. I weep, I pray, but the screams do not stop. I sleep with two pillows. One under my aching head, the other between my thighs. Some mornings I have woken up to find the back-room heroes standing around my mattress on the floor. Standing around and laughing, pointing at the pillow between my withered thighs. I am silent then. I know the day will come when they too seek comfort in ways that seem laughable to others.

When the screams drive me over the edge of despair, when I am tired of weeping and praying, then I remove the pillow between my thighs and press it over my ears. Now the screaming stops.

In the morning I am neglected as usual while the back room comes to life. I open the curtain and look out. I scratch my low-slung onions. Men go about their business. The sun is hot already. There is shame and fatigue on their faces. Since the first night of the scream, I have begun to see this shame and fatigue everywhere. The ones in the back room also wear it.

The dust is thicker today on the furniture. I look in the cold, pitiless mirror. The reflection takes me by surprise. Now I know with certainty: if the others have not already heard the screaming, the time is not far off. Soon it will pierce their beings and rob them of their rest. Their day will come. Their night will come. Poor creatures. My anger towards them is melting. All is forgiven.

The air is still dry, we wait for rain. The beggars have gone on strike. The field are sere, the fish nets empty. The blackmarketeers have begun to hoard. People are filling the temples. The flies are dropping like men.

Mordecai Richler

MY FATHER'S LIFE

The only thing I've been left that was his is a foot-long chisel, which I now keep on a shelf of honor in my workroom. Written with a certain flourish in orange chalk on the oak shaft is his inscription:

USED BY M. I. RICHLER
RICHLER ARTIFICIAL STONE WORKS
1922
DE LA ROCHE STREET
NO SUCCESS

My father was twenty years old then, the eldest of fourteen children. Surely that year, as every year of his life, on Passover he sat in his finery at a dining-room table and recited, 'We were once the slaves of Pharaoh in Egypt, but the Lord our God brought us forth from there with a mighty hand and an outstretched arm.' But come 1922, out in the muck of his father's freezing back yard on de la Roche, yet to absorb the news of his liberation, my father was still trying to make bricks with insufficient straw.

My father, my father.

Insufficient straw, *NO* SUCCESS, was the story of his life. Neither of his marriages really worked. There were searing quarrels with my older brother. As a boy, I made life difficult for him. I had no respect. Later, officious strangers would rebuke him in the synagogue for the novels I had written.

First published in *Esquire*, August 1982.

Heaping calumny on the Jews, they said. If there was such a thing as a reverse Midas touch, he had it. Not one of my father's surefire penny mine stocks ever went into orbit. He never even won a raffle. As younger, more intrepid brothers and cousins began to prosper he assured me, 'The bigger they come, the harder they fall.'

After his marriage to my mother blew apart, he lived alone in a rented room. It was then I discovered that he had a bottle of gin concealed in the glove compartment of his battered Chevy. My father. Gin. 'What's that for?' I asked, astonished.

'For the femmes,' he replied, wiggling his eyebrows at me.

I remember him as a short man with a shiny bald head. Seated at the kitchen table at night in his Penman's long winter underwear, wetting his finger before turning a page of the New York *Daily Mirror*, reading Walter Winchell first. Winchell, who knew what's what. He also devoured *Popular Mechanics, Doc Savage,* and *Black Mask.* His pranks did not enchant my mother. A metal ink spot on her new chenille bedspread. A felt mouse to surprise her in the larder. Neither did his jokes appeal to her. 'Hey, do you know why we eat hard-boiled eggs dipped in salt water just before the Passover meal?'

'No, Daddy. Why?'

'To remind us that when the Jews crossed the Red Sea they certainly got their balls soaked.'

He was stout; he was fleshy. But in his wedding photographs the man who was to become my father is as skinny as I once was, his startled brown eyes unsmiling behind horn-rimmed glasses.

My father never saw Paris. Read Yeats. Or skipped work to make love in the afternoon. What did he hope for? What did he want? Beyond peace and quiet, which he seldom achieved, I have no idea. He never took a risk or was disobedient. At his angriest, I once heard him silence a cousin bragging about his burgeoning real estate investments by saying, 'You know how much land a man needs? Six feet. And one day that's all you'll have. Ha, ha!'

Anticipating Bunker Hunt, my father began to hoard American silver in his rented room. A blue steamer-trunk filling with neatly stacked piles of silver dollars, quarters, dimes. But decades before their worth began to soar, he had to redeem them at face value. He was getting married again. He began to speculate in postage stamps. When he died at the age of sixty-five I also found out that he had bought a city back lot somewhere for twelve hundred dollars sometime during the forties. In 1967, however, its estimated value was nine hundred dollars. All things considered, that called for a real touch of class.

I was charged with appetite. My father had none. I dreamed of winning prizes. He never competed. But, like me, my father was a writer. A keeper of records. His diary, wherein he catalogued injuries and insults, betrayals, family quarrels, was written in a code of his own invention. His brothers and sisters teased him about it, but as cancer began to consume him, they took notice, fluttering about, concerned. 'What about Moishe's diary?'

I wanted it. I felt the diary was my proper inheritance. I hoped it would tell me things about him he had always been too reticent to reveal. But his widow, an obdurate lady, refused to allow me into the locked room in their apartment where he kept his personal papers. All she would allow was, 'I'm returning your mother's love letters to her. The ones he found that time. You know, from the refugee.'

That time would have been the early forties, when my mother began to rent to refugees, putting them up in our spare bedroom. The refugees, German and Austrian Jews, had been interned as enemy aliens in England shortly after war was declared in 1939. They were transported to camps in Canada in 1940. Now they were being released. My father, who had never had anybody to condescend to in his life, was expecting real greeners with side-locks, timorous innocents out of the shtetl, who would look to him as a master of magic. Canadian magic. Instead they turned out to speak better English than any of us did, as well as German and French. After all they had been through, they were still fond of quoting a German son of a bitch called Goethe; they sang opera arias in the bathroom. They didn't guffaw over the antics of Fibber McGee and Molly; neither were they interested in the strippers who worked the Gayety Theatre or in learning how to play gin rummy for a quarter of a cent a point. My mother was enthralled.

My father was afraid of his father. He was afraid of my unhappy mother, who divorced him when I was thirteen. He was also afraid of his second wife. Alas, he was even afraid of me when I was a boy. I rode streetcars on the sabbath. I ate bacon. But nobody was afraid of Moses Isaac Richler. He was far too gentle.

The Richler family was, and remains, joyously Orthodox, followers of the Lubavitcher rabbi. So when my mother threatened divorce, an all-but-unheard-of scandal in its time, grim rabbis in black gaberdine coats hastened to our cold-water flat on St Urbain Street to plead with my mother. But my mother, dissatisfied for years with her arranged marriage, in love at last, was adamant. The rabbis sighed when my father, snapping his suspenders, rocking on his heels, *speaking out*, stated his most deeply felt grievance. When he wakened from his Saturday afternoon nap there was no tea. 'I like a cup of hot tea with lemon when I wake up.'

Weekdays my father wakened every morning at six and drove his truck through the wintry dark to the family scrapyard near the waterfront. He worked there for my fierce, ill-tempered grandfather and a pompous younger brother. Uncle Solly, who had been to high school, had been made a partner in the yard, but not my father, the firstborn. He worked for a salary. Which contributed hugely to my mother's wrath. Younger brothers, determined to escape an overbearing father, had slipped away to form their own business, but my father was too scared to join them. 'When times are bad they'll be back. I remember the Depression. Oh, boy!'

'Tell me about it,' I pleaded.

But my father never talked to me about anything. Not his own boyhood. His feelings. Or his dreams. He never even mentioned sex to me until I was nineteen years old, bound for Paris to try to become a writer. 'You know what safes are. If you have to do it – *and I know you* – use 'em. Don't get married over there. They'd do anything for a Canadian passport.'

He thought I was crazy to sail for Europe, a graveyard for the Jews, a continent where everything was broken or old, but he lent me his blue steamer-trunk and sent me fifty dollars a month support. When I went broke two years later, he mailed me my boat fare home. I told him that the novel I had written over there was called *The Acrobats*, and he immediately suggested that I begin the title of my second novel with a *B*, the third with a *C*, and so on, which would make a nifty trademark for me. Writing, he felt, might not be such a nutty idea after all. He had read in *Life* that this guy Mickey Spillane, a mere goy, was making a fortune. Insulted, I explained hotly that I wasn't that kind of a writer. I was a serious man.

'So?'

'I only write out of my obsessions.'

'Aha,' he said, sighing, warming to me for once, recognizing another generation of family failure.

Even when I was a boy his admonitions were few. 'Don't embarrass me. Don't get into trouble.'

I embarrassed him. I got into trouble.

I caught my grandfather, whom I disliked intensely, giving short weight on his scrapyard scales to a drunken Irish peddler. My grandfather, the religious enforcer. Scornful, triumphant, I told my father the old man was a hypocrite.

'What do you know?' he demanded.

'Nothing,' I said, anticipating.

'They're anti-Semites, every one of them.'

So many things about my father's nature exasperate or mystify me.

All those years he was being crushed by his own father, nagged by my mother, teased (albeit affectionately) by his increasingly affluent brothers and cousins – was he seething inside, plotting vengeance in his diary? Or was he really so sweet-natured as to not give a damn? Finally, there is a possibility I'd rather not ponder. Was he not sweet-natured at all, but a coward. Like me. Who would travel miles to avoid a quarrel. Who tends to remember slights, recording them in my mind's eye, transmogrifying them, finally publishing them in a code more accessible than my father's, that is to say, making them the stuff of fiction.

Riddles within riddles.

My father came to Montreal as an infant, when his father fled Poland. Pogroms. Rampaging cossacks. But, striptease shows aside, the only piece of theater my father relished, an annual outing for the two of us, was the appearance of the Don Cossack Choir at the St Denis Theatre. My father would stamp his foot to their lusty marching and drinking songs. His eyes would light up to see those behemoths, his own father's tormentors, prance onstage. Moses Isaac Richler, who never marched, nor drank, nor pranced.

Obviously he didn't enjoy his family. My mother, my brother, me. Sundays he would usually escape our flat early and alone and start out for the first-run down-town cinemas, beginning with the Princess, which opened earliest, continuing from there to the Capitol or the Palace, and maybe moving on to the Loews, returning to us bleary-eyed but satiated after dark.

My mother was fond of reminding me that the night I was born my father had not waited at the hospital to find out how she was or whether it was a boy or a girl, but had gone to the movies instead. What was playing, I wondered.

Bliss for him was the Gayety Theatre on a Saturday night. My father and a couple of younger brothers, still bachelors, seated front-row center. Onstage, Peaches or the legendary Lili St Cyr. My father rapt, his throat dry, watching the unattainable Lili simulate intercourse with a swan as the stage lights throbbed, then trudging home to sit alone at the kitchen table, drinking hot milk with matzo before going to sleep.

We endured some rough passages together. Shortly after my mother divorced him, I fought with my father. Fists flew. We didn't speak for two years. Then, when we came together again, meeting once a week, it wasn't to talk but to play gin rummy. My father, I began to suspect, wasn't reticent. He didn't understand his life. He had nothing to say to anybody.

In 1956, some time after my return to Europe, where I was to remain rooted for almost two decades, I married a shiksa in London. My father wrote me an indignant letter and we became estranged again. But no sooner did the marriage end in divorce than he pounced, 'You see, mixed marriages never work.'

'But, Daddy, your first marriage didn't work, and Maw was a rabbi's daughter.'

'What do you know?'

'Nothing,' I replied, hugging him.

When I married again, this time for good but to another shiksa, he was not overcome with delight, but neither did he complain. For, after all the wasting years, we had finally become friends. I had endeared myself to him in the only way possible. My father became my son. Once he sent money to me in Paris. Now, as the scrapyard foundered, I mailed monthly checks to him in Montreal. On visits home I took him to restaurants. I bought him treats.

What I'm left with are unresolved mysteries. A sense of regret. Anecdotes for burnishing. My wife, a proud lady, showing him our firstborn son, his week-old howling grandchild, saying, 'Don't you think he looks like Mordecai?'

'Babies are babies,' he responded, sighing, indifferent.

Some years later my father coming to our house, pressing chocolate bars on the kids. 'Who do you like better,' he asked them, 'your father or your mother?'

In the late sixties, I flew my father to London. He came with his wife. Instead of slipping away with him to the Windmill Theatre or another strip joint, like a fool I acquired theater tickets. We took the two of them to that memorable satirical revue *Beyond the Fringe*. 'What do you think?' I asked as we left the theater.

'There was no chorus line,' he said.

After his last operation for cancer I flew to Montreal, promising to take him on a trip as soon as he was out of bed. The Catskills. Grossinger's. With a stopover in New York to take in some shows. But each time I phoned from London his doctor advised me to wait a bit longer. I waited. He died. The next time I flew to Montreal it was to bury him.

Olive Senior

YOU THINK I MAD, MISS?

You think I mad, Miss? You see me here with my full head of hair and my notebook and pencil, never go out a street without my stockings straight and shoes shine good for is so my mother did grow me. Beg you a smalls, nuh? Then why your face mek up so? Don't I look like somebody pickney? Don't I look like teacher? Say what? Say why I living on street then? Then is who tell you I living on street? See here, is Sheraton I live. All them box and carochies there on the roadside? Well, I have to whisper and tell you this for I don't want the breeze to catch it. You see the wappen-bappen on the streetside there? Is one old lady ask me to watch it for her till she come back. And cause mi heart so good, me say yes. I watching it day and night though is Sheraton I live. For the old lady don't come back yet. Quick before the light change for I don't eat nutten from morning. I don't know is what sweet you so. But thank you all the same. Drive good, you hear.

I hope you don't hear already, Sar, what that foolish Doctor Bartholomew saying about me all over town? Is him should lock up in Bellevue and all the people inside there set free, you know. But he couldn't keep me lock up for I smarter than all of them. That's what Teacher used to tell me. I come brighter than all the other pickney around. And tree never grow in my face neither. Beg you a little food money there nuh before the light turn green. A who you calling dutty? A why you a wind up yu

This story is taken from the collection *Discerner of Hearts* (1995).

window and mek up yu face? You know say is Isabella Francina Myrtella Jones this you a talk to? And since when dutty bwoy like you think you can eggs-up so talk to Miss Catherine daughter that studying to turn teacher? Why you a turn yu head a gwan seh you no see me? I know you see me all right for, though I don't behave as if I notice, I know all you young men sitting on the bridge every day there eyeing me as I pass. Would like to drag me down, drag me right down to your level. Have my name outa road like how you all have Canepiece Icilda. And that is why I hold up my head and wear two slip under my skirt. And I don't pay you all no mind. For what I would want with any of you? Then wait, you not even giving me a two cents there and I don't eat from morning? Gwan, you ol' red nayga you. From I see you drive up I shoulda know seh is that Bartholomew send you. Send you to torment me. You ugly just like him, to rah. Go weh!

Hello, my sweet little darling. What you have to give me today? I don't eat a thing from morning, Mother. I wouldn't tell you lie in front of your little girl. Is same so my little one did look, you know? Seven pound, six and a half ounce she did weigh, and pretty like a picture. Is bad-minded people make them take her away. Thank you, Mother. God bless you and the little darling. Say who take her? Well me have to whisper it for me don't want the breeze to catch it. But is that Elfraida Campbell, that's who. The one that did say me did grudge her Jimmy Watson. Then you nuh remember her? Is she and her mother burn bad candle for me mek me buck mi foot and fall. For I never had those intentions. No such intentions. Is two slip I wear under my skirt for I was studying to be teacher. Is Miss Catherine my mother, you know. Say the light changing? You gone? God bless you, my precious daughter.

Young girl, I see you courting. But don't mek that young man behind steering wheel have business with you before you married, you hear? For once he know you he drag you down, drag you down to nutten. Then is pure ashes you eat. Pure dutty fe yu bed. The two of you a laugh! You better mind is nuh laugh today, cry tomorrow. But what a way you resemble Jimmy Watson ee? Him was handsome just like you. Thank you, mi darling, the two of you drive good, you hear. Say who is Jimmy Watson? Then you never know him? The same Jimmy Watson that did come as the assistant teacher and all the girls did love him off. Well, not me. For I didn't have no intention to take on young man before I get certification. Is Shortwood Teacher Training College I was going to, you know. Eh-eh, then you just wind up yu window and drive off so? What a bad-mannered set of children ee!

Like I was saying, Sar, I was busy with my studying and that is why that Elfraida Campbell did get her hooks into Jimmy Watson. For what Jimmy would really want with girl that can barely sign her name, nuh matter she walk and fling her hips about? So I just study and bide my time. Oh, God bless you, Sar, I could kiss yu hand. Is from morning I don't eat, you know. But that Elfraida is such a wicked girl, Sar, she and her mammy. If you ever see her, please call the constable for me, for is plenty things she have to answer for. Courthouse business, Sar. If she and her mammy didn't work negromancy on me, Doctor Batholomew wouldn't be looking for me all now. But he will never never find me. You want to know why? You see that big box there a roadside? Is there I hide, you know. Once I get inside my box, not a living soul can find me. They could send out one million policeman to search for me. Two million soldier. The whole of Salvation Army. They could look into the box till they turn fool. They could shine they torch, bring searchlight and X-ray and TV and atomic bomb. Not one of them could ever find me. Aright, Sar. You gone? God bless you.

Look at my darling lady in the white car who always give me something. God bless you and keep you, my dear. Mine how you travel, you hear? Satan set plenty snares in the world for the innocent. Take me, now. Is not me did go after Jimmy Watson. As God is mi judge. Him and Elfraida Campbell was getting on good-good there. It was a disgrace that a girl should act so common and make people carry her name all over the district like that. Even the breeze did tek it. And he was man of education too. What about his reputation? So when he first put question to me I didn't business, for I never want people have anything to say about me and I don't get my certificate yet. But it was just as I thought. Jimmy Watson wanted a woman that wouldn't shame him, a decent woman with broughtupcy and plenty book-learning. That is how he put it to me. And I resist and I resist but, after a while, that Jimmy Watson so handsome and have sweet-mout so, him confabulation just wear down mi resistance. Never mind bout certification and teacher college – eh-eh, you gone already. God bless you, sweetheart.

Sar, you see that police fellow there from morning? The constable that is like a thorn in mi side? Can't get a good night rest from him beating on mi bedroom with him stick. Is what do him ee? Is Satan send him to torment me, you know. You know who Satan is? Beg you a dollar, nuh? A hungry, you see. A don't eat a thing from morning. Satan and Bartholomew is one and the same. Then you never know? And you look so bright? Look as if is university you come from. Don't is so? Well, thank you, Sar. The good Lord will bless you. And if you see Bartholomew there up at U. C., tell him is lie. Is lie he telling about the baby. Say it was all in mi mind. You ever hear a piece of madness like that? Is Bartholomew they suppose to lock up and the child weigh eight and three-quarter pound? A spanking baby boy. Is that cause Elfraida Campbell to burn bad candle for me. Jealousy just drive her crazy. Eh-hm. Drive good, ya. And beg you tell government what Bartholomew going on with, you hear?

From I born and grow I never know man could lie like that Jimmy Watson. Is only Bartholomew lie good like him, you know, my lady and gentleman. Thank you for a smalls, Sar, for a cup of tea. Nothing pass my lips from morning. Thank you, Sar. God bless. You did know Jimmy Watson swear to my mother he never touch me? Never have a thing to do with me? Fancy that! So is who was lying with me every night there? Who was plunging into me like St George with his sword? He cry the living eye-water the day my mother ask if he business with me, for that time the baby already on the way. I could feel it kicking inside me. And that lying Jimmy Watson say he never lay hands on me. Same thing the lying Bartholomew did tell my mother. That no man ever touch me. How man can lie so ee? So is how the baby did come then, answer me that? How baby can born so, without father? Ten and a half pound it weigh. Say what, Sar? Say why if I have children I living on street? Then is why unno red nayga so faas and facety ee? Answer me that. You see me asking you question bout fe yu pickney? Unno gwan! Think because you see me look so I don't come from nowhere? Ever see me without my paper and pencil yet? Ever see me without my shoes and stocking and two slip under my dress? Think I wear them little clingy-clingy frock without slip like that Elfraida Campbell so every man could see my backside swing when I walk? Unno gwan!

So is what sweet you so, you little facety bwoy? You never see stone fling after car yet? You want me bus one in yu head? Say somebody shoulda call police? So why you don't do it, since you so shurance and force-ripe? Mek that constable bwoy come near me today. Mek them send that Bartholomew. Send for them. Do. I want them to arrest me at Lady Musgrave Road traffic light here today. I want them to take me down to court-house. I want to have my day in court. I want to stand up in front of judge and jury. I want to say 'Justice' and beg him to ask them certain question. He-hey. Don't mek I laugh here today. You want to know something, sweet bwoy. Them not going to do a thing about me, you know. Say wha mek? Well, me have to whisper it, for me nuh want no breeze catch hold of it. But the reason is because they fraid. Fraid to give me my day in court. Fraid to have me ask my question there. All of them fraid. Even the judge. Even Massa God himself. For nobody want to take responsibility to answer me. Gwan, you little dutty bwoy. Yu face favour!

Good day, Missis. You did say you want to hear my question? Well, beg you a money there nuh, please. I don't get a thing to eat from morning. Thank you, Miss. You want to hear my question, please? So why you winding up yu glass? Why you unmannersable so? Well, whether you want to hear or not, you stupid bitch, I, Isabella Francina Myrtella Jones, am going to tell you. So you can ease down all you want. I going to shout it from Lady Musgrave Road traffic light. I going to make the breeze take it to the four corners of everywhere. First: Is who take away my child? Second: Why Jimmy Watson lie so and say he never lie with me? Third: Why they let that Elfraida Campbell and her mother tie Jimmy Watson so I never even have a chance with him? Fourth: Why my mother Miss Catherine never believe anything I say again. Why she let me down so? Is obeah them obeah her too why she hand me over to that Bartholomew? Fifth: Why that Bartholomew madder than mad and he walking bout free as a bird? Who give him the right to lock up people in Bellevue and burn bright light all night and ask them all sort of foolish question? Sixth: What is the government going to do about these things? Seventh: If there is still Massa God up above, is what I do why him have to tek everybody side against me?

Vikram Seth

NEEM

Profiting

Uncomprehending day,
I tie my loss to leaves
And watch them drift away.

The regions are as far,
But the whole quadrant sees
The single generous star.

Yet under star or sun,
For forest tree or leaf
The year has wandered on.

And for the single cells
Held in their sentient skins
An image shapes and tells:

In wreathes of ache and strain
The bent rheumatic potter
Contructs his forms from pain.

The They

They have left me the quiet gift of fearing.
I am consumed by fear, chilling and searing.

I shiver at night. I cannot sleep. I burn
By night, by day. I tremble. They return.

They bear an abstract laser to destroy
Love-love and Live-live, little girl and boy.

Thus my heart jolts in fear. For they are known
To liquidate the squealers, sparing none.

Needless to say, the death is always long.
I weep to think of it; I am not strong.

Who are the They? Why do they act this way?
Some of us know, but no-one dares to say.

The Comfortable Classes at Work and Play

A squirrel crawls on top of Ganesh.
Oscar turns over on his stomach and rolls about.
Seven satbhai-champas chatter and burble below the bignonia
    trellis.
The raat-ki-rani and malati and harsingar mingle their scent.
Above, two crows on the eaves upset Divali diyas on the
    ground,
And in the evening a hoopoe pecks at the lawn
While mynahs frolic at the edge of the mango's shade
And parrots flash across the sky.

Early in the morning the mew-like wail
Of peacocks from the grounds of Nehru's old house,
Now the Teenmurti Library, comes down the lanes,
And down the lanes and across the garden hedges
The peacocks themselves, turquoise-necked, turquoise-breasted
(With tail-feathers all robbed to make peacock fans)
Walk primly to our neighbours' houses and ours
Conducting a progress through the vegetable garden.

Sona the gardener does not chase them out
From by the banana tree and the gourd-vines.
He prunes the roses, the hedge, the champa, the two

Lantana elephants that welcome walkers in
To walk, after drinking ginger tea against the chill,
In chappals on the dew-soft dew-greyed lawn
Or to sit on the large white swing
And swing and stare or read.

The eldest son brings down his surpeti
And mumbles a snatch of Lalit, then hums and lapses.
Oscar bores out of the hedge from the neighbour's garden
And hurls himself barking at the singer's feet.
The eldest son says, 'No, Oscar, no!'
But is persuaded by a sequence of short nips
To run Oscar down the red path
As far as the whitewashed gate.

The second son brings down *The Women's Room,*
Of Woman Born, My Mother/My Self and *Sexual Politics.*
His girl-friend is feminist, and he is feminist.
When his girl-friend was anarchist, he was anarchist.
He has begun of late to talk in psychobabble
And his elder brother does not improve energy interflows
By cynical imitation of his style of speech
Or cynical puncturing of his current ism.

The daughter of the house sits in her room
Immersed in sociology and social visits
Paid her at any hour by many friends,
And talks about their coming field-trip south
Where they, like earlier cohorts from their college
('A shock of sociologists') will examine
The much-examined customs of the Todas
(Who have learned now to exploit their data-pickers).

In the long sunlit closed verandah
The mother takes a volume in half-calf
From off the wall, and wrestles with a judgment
Of Justice Krishna Iyer of the Supreme Court.
He must mean something, but what does he mean?
'The endless pathology of factious scrimmage' – and now
'Crypto-coercion'. She knits her forehead
And asks for another cup of ginger tea.

The father sits in bed reading the *Indian Express*,
Inveighing against politicians and corruption.
'India could do so much . . .' he says.
'Even in the time of the British . . .' he says.
'Can you believe it – on every bag of cement –
And still he continues to be a minister!
The rot has gone too deep. Let's go for a walk.'
He and the elder son drive to Lodi gardens.

There against the exquisite morning sky
The Arab domes of the tombs sit formed and fine
And neem and semal, ashok and amaltas
And casuarina lend the air freshness, the heart peace.
On the enamel-striped domes the vultures nest.
Along the casual paths three joggers thump.
A group of eight old citizens wearing safas
Gossip in the growing sun and laugh with abandon.

At home the grandmother has sat down to breakfast
And complains that she is ignored, unloved.
Her blood pressure is high, her spirits low.
She is not allowed to eat gulabjamuns.
The doctor has compiled an Index of Foods
And today, to compound things, is a non-grain fast.
Her dentures hurt. She looks at a stuffed tomato
And considers how to darn her grandson's sweater.

The Gift

Awake, he recalls
The district of his sleep.
It was desert land,
The dunes gold, steep,
Warm to the bare foot, walls
Of pliant sand.

Someone, was he a friend?,
Placed a stone of jade
In his hand
And, laughing, said

'When this comes to an end
You will not understand.'

He is awake, yet through
The ache of light
He longs to dream again.
He longs for night,
The contour of the sand, the rendezvous,
The gift of jade, of sight.

Homeless

I envy those
Who have a house of their own,
Who can say their feet
Rest on what is theirs alone,
Who do not live on sufferance
In strangers' shells,
As my family has all our life,
And as I probably will.

A place on the earth, untenured,
Soil, grass, brick, air;
To know I will never have to move;
To review the seasons from one lair.
When night comes, to lie down in peace;
To know that I may die as I have slept;
That things will not revert to a stranger's hand;
That those I love may keep what I have kept.

From the Babur-Nama
Memoirs of Babur, First Moghul Emperor of India

I.

A lad called Baburi lived in the camp-bazaar.
Odd how our names matched. I became fond of him –
'Nay, to speak truth, distracted after him.'

I had never before this been in love
Or witnessed words expressive of passion, but now
I wrote some Persian verses: 'Never was lover
So wretched, so enamoured, so dishonoured
As I'; and others of this type. Sometimes
Baburi came to see me, and I, Babur,
Could scarcely look him in the face, much less
Talk to him, amuse him, or disclose the matter
Weighing on me. So joyful was I I could not
Thank him for visiting; how then could I
Reproach him for departing? I lacked even
The self-command to be polite to him.
Passing one day through a narrow lane with only
A few companions, suddenly, face to face,
I met him, and I almost fell to pieces.
I could not meet his eyes or say a word.
Shame overcame me. I passed on, and left him,
And Muhammed Salih's verses came to my mind –
'I am abashed whenever I see my love.
My friends look at me; I look another way.'

This passion in my effervescent youth
Drove me through lane and street, bare-foot, bare-headed,
Through orchard, vineyard, neglecting the respect
And attention due both to myself and to others:
'During my passion I was deranged, nor knew that
Such is the state of one who is in love.'
Sometimes, afflicted, I would roam alone
Over the mountains and deserts, sometimes I wandered
From street to street, in suburbs and in gardens.
'To such a state did you reduce me, O heart – '
I could not stand or walk; remain or go.

2.

At dawn we left the stream and resumed our march.
I ate a maajun. Under its effect
I visited some gardens, dense with yellow
And purple flowers; some beds yellow, some purple,
And some so intermingled – sprung up together
As if they had been flung and scattered abroad.
I sat down on a hillock. On every side

The gardens lay before me, shaped into beds,
Yellow on one side, purple on another,
Laid out in hexagons, exquisitely.

On Saturday we had a drinking party.
The following day, when we had nearly arrived
At Khwajeh Sehyaran, a serpent was killed,
As thick as an arm, as long as two outstretched.
Out of this large one crept a thinner one,
Yet all its parts were sound and quite uninjured;
Out of this thinner serpent came a mouse,
Perfectly sound again, with no limb injured.
(When we arrived, we had a drinking party.)

Hindustan is a land of meagre pleasures.
The people are not handsome, nor have they
The least conception of the charms of friendship.
They have no spirit, no comprehension, kindness
Or fellow-feeling – no inventiveness
In handicraft or skill in design – no method,
Order, principle, rule in work or thought;
No good flesh or bread in their bazaars,
No ice, cold water, musk-melons, grapes; no horses;
No aqueducts or canals in palace or garden,
Not a single bath or college in the whole land,
No candles, no torches; not even a candlestick.

A splendid bird, more known for colour and beauty
Than bulk, is the peacock. Its size is that of the crane.
The head of the male has an iridescent lustre;
His neck is a fine blue, his back is rich
With yellows, violets, greens and blues, and stars
Extend to the very extremity of his tail.
The bird flies badly, worse indeed than the pheasant:
Where peacocks choose to live, jackals abound.
The doctrines of Hanifeh state that the bird
Is lawful food, its flesh quite pleasant, quail-like;
But eaten somewhat with loathing – like that of the camel.

The frogs of Hindustan are worthy of notice.
Although their species is the same as ours,
They will run seven yards on the face of the water.

3.

Noblemen and soldiers – every man
Who comes into this world is subject to
Dissolution. When we pass away
God alone survives, unchangeable.
Whoever tastes the feast of life must drink
The cup of death. The traveller at the inn
Of mortality sooner or later leaves
That house of sorrow, the world. Is it not better
To die with honour than live with infamy?
'With fame, even to die makes me content.
Let me have fame, since Death has my body.'
The Most High God has been propitious to us
For we are placed in such a crisis that
Should we now die we die the death of martyrs
And should we live we will have served his cause.
Let us all swear then not to turn from battle
Nor desert the slaughter ensuing until we die.

4.

To Humayun, whom I long to see; much health.
On Saturday your letters came from the Northwest.
Praise be to God, who has given you a child;
To you a child, to me an object of love
And comfort. You name him Al Amaan. Consider,
'The protected' – Al Amaan – is pronounced by some
Alaaman, which means 'plunderer' in our tongue!
Well, may God prosper his name and constitution;
May he be happy, and we made happy by
The fame and fortune of Al Amaan. Indeed
God from his grace and bounty has accomplished
Most unprecedentedly all our desires.

On the eleventh I heard the men of Balkh
Had opened the city. I sent word to your brother
And to the Begs to join you against Merv,
Hissar or Samarkand as you deem fittest,
That through God's mercy you might be enabled
To scatter the enemy, seize their lands, and make
Your friends rejoice in their discomfiture.
This is the time to expose yourself to danger.

Exort yourself, and meet things as they come,
For indolence suits ill with royalty.
If through God's favour Balkh and Hissar are ours,
You rule Hissar; let Kamran be in Balkh.
If Samarkand should fall, it falls to you.
Six parts are always yours, and five Kamran's;
Remember this; the great are generous.

I have a quarrel with you. Your letters are
Illegible. They take hours to decode –
The writing crabbed, the style, too, somewhat strange.
(A riddle is not normally written in prose.)
The spelling is not bad (though *iltafaat*
Is spelt with *te* not *toeh*); yet even when read
The far-fetched diction you delight in veils
Your meaning. This is affectation. Write
From now on, clearly, using words that cost
Less torment both to your reader and to you.

In several of your letters you are saddened
By separation from your friends. Consider –
'If you are independent, follow your will.
If circumstances fetter you, submit.'
There is no bondage greater than a king's.
Of this, my son, do not therefore complain.

This letter goes to you with Bian Sheikh
Who will tell you much else by word of mouth.
Maintain the army's discipline and force.
Farewell. The thirteenth day of the first Rabi.

5.

Humayun left Badakhshan after a year,
Journeying via Kabul to Agra to see me.
He sent no word. His mother and I were talking
Of him when he appeared. His presence made
Our hearts blossom like rosebuds, and our eyes shine
Like torches. It had been my daily custom
To hold an open table, yet when he arrived
I threw a feast in his honour and treated him
In both a distinguished and most intimate manner.

The truth is that his conversation held
An inexpressible charm, and he realised
For me the very type of the perfect man.

When the time came Humayun took his leave
To go to Sambhal, his appointed seat,
Where he remained six months. He became ill.
The climate did not suit him. Fever attacked him
And worsened daily. I ordered that he be brought
To Agra, so the best doctors might prescribe
Some treatment. He travelled by water several days.
Despite the remedies he got no better.
His life was despaired of. I was in despair
Till Abdul Kasim said, 'In such a case
A sacrifice of great value may incline God
To restore the patient's health.' Nothing was dearer
Than his life save my own. I offered it.
My friends protested, saying the great diamond
That came to me with Agra would suffice.
I entered the chamber where my son was lying
And circled his bed three times, saying each time,
'I take upon myself all that you suffer.'
I forthwith felt myself depressed and heavy
And in much pain. He rose in perfect health.
I called my noblemen. Placing their hands
In Humayun's as a mark of investiture,
I proclaimed him heir and placed him on the throne.
Those there concurred, and bound themselves to serve him.

WINNERS OF THE COMMONWEALTH WRITERS PRIZE 1987–1996

1987   *winner*: Olive Senior
runner-up: Witi Ihimaera

1988   *winner*: Festus Iyayi
runner-up: George Turner

1989   *winner*: Janet Frame
best first book: Bonnie Burnard

1990   *winner*: Mordecai Richler
best first book: John Cranna

1991   *winner*: David Malouf
best first book: Pauline Melville

1992   *winner*: Rohinton Mistry
best first book: Robert Antoni

1993   *winner*: Alex Miller
best first book: Githa Hariharan

1994   *winner*: Vikram Seth
best first book: Keith Oatley

1995   *winner*: Louis de Bernières
best first book: Adib Khan

1996   *winner*: Rohinton Mistry
best first book: Vikram Chandra

BIOGRAPHICAL NOTES

AMA ATA AIDOO was born in Ghana in 1942. She is regarded as one of Africa's leading feminist writers. She first came to prominence with a play, *The Dilemma of a Ghost* (1964). A collection of short stories, *No Sweetness Here*, was published in 1970; her fiction includes *Our Sister Killjoy* (1977) and *Changes* (1992), which won the Africa Best Book section of the Commonwealth Writers Prize. Aidoo has written two volumes of poetry, *Someone Talking to Sometime* (1985) and *An Angry Letter in Jaunuary* (1992). She was formerly Minister of Education in Ghana.

LOUIS DE BERNIÈRES lives in London. His first two novels won regional Commonwealth Prizes, *The War of Don Emmanuel's Nether Parts* and *Señor Vivo and the Coca Lord*. He was selected as one of the 20 Best of Young British Novelists in 1993, and *Captain Corelli's Mandolin* won the Commonwealth Writers Prize in 1995.

LINDSEY COLLEN was born in 1943 in the Transkei in South Africa. She has been based in Mauritius for many years and is a civil activist. Her first novel, *There is a Tide*, was published in 1990. Her second, *The Rape of Sita* (1993), won the Africa Best Book section of the Commonwealth Writers Prize in 1994, and was immediately taken up by the Heinemann African Writers Series, though the Mauritian government banned it on account of its alleged religious offensiveness.

JOHN CRANNA was born in New Zealand in 1954 and grew up in the Waikato. He spent a number of years in London and now lives in Auckland, where he works for the New Zealand Human Rights Commission. *Visitors* won the 1990 New Zealand Book Award for Fiction, and the 1990 Commonwealth Writers Prize for Best First Book. His novel *Arena* was published in 1992.

GITHA HARIHARAN lives in New Delhi, where she works as a freelance editor. Her first novel, *The Thousand Faces of Night* (1992) won the Commonwealth Writers Prize for Best First Book. She has published a collection of stories, *The Art of Dying* (1993) and a novel, *The Ghosts of Vasu Master* (1994). She has also edited *A Southern Harvest*, a volume of stories in English translation from four major South Indian languages.

ADIB KHAN was born in Dhaka, Bangladesh, where he lived until 1973. He then went to Australia and completed a Masters Degree in English Literature at Monash University. He is currently a teacher in Ballarat. His first novel, *Seasonal Adjustments*, won several awards including the Commonwealth Writers Prize for Best First Book (1995). His second novel is *Solitude of Illusions* (1996).

PAULINE MELVILLE is of Guyanese and British descent. *Shape-Shifter*, her first collection of stories, won the Guardian Fiction Prize, the Macmillan Silver Pen Award and the Commonwealth Writers' Prize for Best First Book (1991). Her first novel, *The Ventriloquist's Tale*, is due to be published by Bloomsbury in 1997.

ALEX MILLER lives in Melbourne and is currently Visiting Fellow at La Trobe University, and has a Senior Fellowship from the Australia Council. His third novel, *The Ancestor Game* (1992) won both the Miles Franklin Literary Award and the Commonwealth Writers Prize, and has been translated into Mandarin. He is working on his fifth novel, *The Conditions of Faith*.

ROHINTON MISTRY was born in Bombay in 1952 and immigrated to Canada in 1975. He is the author of *Tales from Firozsha Baag*, a collection of short stories. His first novel, *Such a Long Journey* (1991), was shortlisted for the Booker Prize, won the Governor General's Award, the Commonwealth Writers Prize for Best Book, and the SmithBooks/*Book in Canada* First Novel Award. His second novel, *A Fine Balance* (1995), won the Giller Prize, the Commonwealth Writers Prize, and was shortlisted for the Booker Prize. Rohinton Mistry was also the recipient of the 1995 Canada-Australia Literary Award.

MORDECAI RICHLER was born in Montreal in 1931, and published his first novel, *The Acrobats*, in 1954. His many awards include the Commonwealth Writers Prize (1990) for his novel *Solomon Gursky Was Here*. He has most recently published a memoir, *This Year in Jerusalem*.

OLIVE SENIOR, a Jamaican educated in Jamaica and Canada, is the author of eight books including the short-story collection *Summer Lightning* (1986), which won the Commonwealth Writers Prize. Her latest publications are *Gardening in the Tropics* (poetry, 1994) and *Discerner of Hearts* (short stories, 1995), and she was recently Distinguished International Writer at St Lawrence University, New York.

VIKRAM SETH was born in Calcutta. He was trained as an economist and has lived for several years each in the UK, California, China and India. He has published three volumes of poetry, *Mappings, The Humble Administrator's Garden*, and *All You Who Sleep Tonight*; a volume of translations from Classical Chinese, *Three Chinese Poets*; a book of verse fables, *Beastly Tales from Here and There*; and a libretto for the opera *Arion and the Dolphin*. He is also the author of *From Heaven Lake: Travels through Sinkiang and Tibet, The Golden Gate: A Novel in Verse*, and the novel, *A Suitable Boy*, which won the Commonwealth Writers Prize (1994).

ACKNOWLEDGEMENTS

AMA ATA AIDOO. 'About the Wedding Feast'. Copyright © Ama Ata Aidoo 1997. Published with permission.

LOUIS DE BERNIERES. 'Stupid Gringo'. Copyright © Louis de Bernieres 1997. Published with permission.

LINDSEY COLLEN. 'The Company I Keep', first published in Barien Pyamootoo and Rama Poonoosamy (eds), *Maurice: Demain et Après, Beyond Tomorrow, Apredimé*, Mauritius, 1996. Copyright © Lindsey Collen 1996. Reprinted with permission.

JOHN CRANNA. 'Visitors' from *Visitors*, first published by Reed Books (Auckland) 1989. Copyright © John Cranna 1989. Reprinted with permission.

GITHA HARIHARAN. Extract from *The Ghosts of Vasu Master*, first published by Viking Penguin (India) 1994. Copyright © Githa Hariharan 1994. Reprinted with permission.

ADIB KHAN. 'Rainbow Voices' from a novel-in-progress. Copyright © Adib Khan 1997. Published with permission.

PAULINE MELVILLE. 'A Quarrelsome Man', first published in *Shape-Shifter* by Picador 1990. Copyright © Pauline Melville 1990. Reprinted with permission.

ALEX MILLER. Extract from *The Sitters*, first published by Viking (Australia) 1995. Copyright © Alex Miller 1995. Reprinted with permission.

ROHINTON MISTRY. 'The Scream', first published in *Soho Square* by Bloomsbury 1994. Copyright © Rohinton Mistry 1994. Reprinted with permission.

MORDECAI RICHLER. 'My Father's Life', first published in *Esquire*, August 1982. Copyright © Mordecai Richler 1982. Reprinted with permission.

OLIVE SENIOR. 'You Think I Mad, Miss?', first published in *Discerner of Hearts*, 1995. Copyright © Olive Senior 1995. Used by permission of McClelland & Stewart, Inc., Toronto, the Canadian publishers.

VIKRAM SETH. 'Neem', first published in *The Humble Administrator's Garden* by Carcanet Press 1985. Copyright © Vikram Seth 1985. Reprinted with permission.